PETER COOK

RORY FLYN
Croyardhill
BEAULY IV4 7EX

PRIMER

A.D. ACADEMY EDITIONS

This book is dedicated to my wife Yael and son Alexander, seen here experiencing architecture at the hand of my friend Enric Miralles.

The author would like to extend his profound thanks to Laura Allen who has energetically helped make this book happen, to Sarah Wigglesworth and Jeremy Till who allowed him to raid their slide collection, and to Maggie Toy and Lucy Ryan at Academy who made the whole process so relaxing.

COVER AND PAGE 1, FROM ABOVE LEFT TO RIGHT: Shonandai Cultural Centre, Itsuko Hasegawa, 1988 (detail); Spiral Housing, Zvi Hecker, Ramat-Gan near Tel Aviv; Palm House, Volker Giencke, Graz, Austria (completed 1994); Glass Bridge, Peter Rice and Ian Ritchie, Paris, 1985

First published in Great Britain in 1996 by
ACADEMY EDITIONS
An imprint of

ACADEMY GROUP LTD
42 Leinster Gardens, London W2 3AN
Member of the VCH Publishing Group

ISBN 1 85490 388 8

Distributed to the trade in the United States of America by
NATIONAL BOOK NETWORK, INC
4720 Boston Way, Lanham, Maryland 20706

Printed and bound in Singapore

CONTENTS

ARCHITECTURE AS A DISCUSSION

The Regard of Architecture

Those of us with real enthusiasm for architecture become as partisan as any football fan, as conscious of mannerisms and style as any music lover and as eager to spot vintage characteristics in the work of our favourite architects as the most persistent wine connoisseur. Like these fellow fanatics, we layer this enthusiasm upon itself and become steadily detached from the everyday cynicism with which we observe other things. We become deaf, if puzzled, by the mildest enquiries as to why we find a certain building special. We may become irritated by those who prefer alternative sets of mannerisms, styles and questioning. We question; we have to spell out the criteria. Suddenly we are exposed.

Unlike those territories where performance can be measured – such as in a race or an achievable feat – there is little that can be proved. Architectural criteria and the assembly of evidence is difficult to verify (in the scientific sense) and thus its very empiricism becomes either quaint, coy or fascinating to the outside observer. On reflection, the apparent inconsequentiality of architectural values and the wide range of criteria have created difficulties that are paralleled in the cultural vortex of a world where value for money and packaged information are tantamount. In periods of cultural stress there is little room for complexity or waywardness.

Yet it is these very characteristics that hint at the quality of the pursuit. In the following pages I will deliberately move back and forth between observational and operational matters and between measurable and immeasurable observations. In doing so I may be able to assemble criteria of a kind; but the delight as well as the irritation of architecture is to be found in this mixture, this open-endedness. The straightforward approach is to see 'what is there', and the layman quite reasonably reckons that he can comment on an artefact that he passes on a daily basis. Herein lies the central problem of architectural discussion: how to involve all the byways of sensibility into a recognisable pattern, and how this pattern can read against 'reality'.

Going back into medieval times, there must have been a sufficient state of useful hearsay for a team of cathedral builders to track across Europe and have

Tokyo street scene

Tamana City Observatory Museum, Masaharu Takasaki, 1987 (project subsequently built)

Project from '101 Fantasies', Jacob Chernikhov, 1928

at its head an identifiable Master Craftsman such as St Hugh at Lincoln Cathedral. It is not until the Age of Enlightenment, or the eighteenth century in Europe, that a new type of character emerged, somewhat removed from the business of actual craftsmanship but able, in a detached way, to apply objective values and measures by placing pieces of craftwork together in a seemly manner.

I am referring now to the phenomenon of the 'Gentleman' architect who was not necessarily a *dilettante* personality (Christopher Wren was, after all, a noted scientist, Thomas Jefferson a National President and Thomas Hardy remembered for his Romantic characters rather than his rural houses). Yet, somehow, architecture emerged as a pleasant pursuit, both useful and vaguely 'artistic', and this mythology has persisted almost up to the present day. Indeed, we might pause to reflect upon the characterisation that is given to architecture in different cultures by the way of its absorption into the universities. The survival of a division between the Academies of Art and the Technology or Engineering Department is still a divide in those cities that are active architecturally and the way in which debate is held still subscribes occasionally to the idea that the Engineers or Technologists 'get the job done' and the Academics 'discuss higher things'. Such notions served architecture poorly, reinforcing the detachment of the man in the street who might discuss the size and type of a window with the engineer/architect and keep well away from the vagaries of the 'Academy' type. It avoids the issue that in the last one hundred years, architecture and architectural philosophy have developed far further in the direction of technique-driven ideas than in the reiteration of mystical 'art' values. Or, to take another view, that 'art' lies in the engineering. In order to deal with this new architecture we must develop a new set of values that will be capable of recognising quality of idea through quality of the resultant environment in addition to arrangement of identifiable objects.

Six Popular Buildings

It might be worth discussing the following six buildings not in terms of their ultimate viability as buildings, nor by trying to evaluate their true worth in relation to other buildings or even other buildings of their period or type, but simply by attempting to elucidate the matured enjoyment that they give. By doing so we might gain an insight into the true relationship that the general public has with architecture. The list consists of: The Taj Mahal in Agra, St Basil's Cathedral in Moscow, the Chrysler Building in New York, the Houses of Parliament in London, the Pompidou Centre in Paris and Sydney Opera House. Clearly, they are all major monumental edifices and most of them are in great cities; however, it is here that the similarity ends.

The Taj Mahal, Agra

The Mausoleum is a seventeenth-century tomb built for the Mumtaz-I-Mahal, wife of Emperor Shah Jehan. Its perfectly placed large Islamic dome is copiously held on four complex octagon towers. The deep recessed arches are a comprehensible symbol of substance. The whole mass is white and iconic; but there is sufficient indication of 'fineness' in the detail that it is not necessary to identify all its components. One must remember that 99 per cent of the Taj Mahal's admirers see no more than a photograph of it. It is readable as a three-dimensional fretwork myth.

St Basil's Cathedral, Moscow (sixteenth century)

The cathedral is adorned with eight domes, their bulbous heads each individually marked, coloured and divided. A building of great exuberance although in today's terms, the extravagance seems almost absurd and therefore (presumably) questionable. Yet at the same time it is composed with a certain elegance and is entirely successful in pronouncing simultaneously the richness, zeal and sophistication of the church. The overall effect is entirely welcoming in a secular sense.

Chrysler Building, New York City (twentieth century)

In the context of hundreds of towers and without typological distinction, this building is memorable as a face in the same way as a person of average size and deportment could be memorable as a face. Few architects have realised the importance of the identification of the head of the tower so brilliantly. Of course, the head does send buttresses down to the ground and the stylisation is pitched at a scale that makes it readable down the block and even further. This building understood its *milieu* exactly.

Houses of Parliament, London (nineteenth century): Planning architect, Sir Charles Barry; decorating architect, Augustus Welby Pugin

The continuity of the detail, which seems totally to dominate the occurrence of windows, is able to create a general sense of richness without the specification of events – except for the key outcrop of the clock tower (Big Ben) at the eastern end, the massive Victoria Tower at the western end and the lighter, more elusive tower. There is not too much for the general public to digest and the Tudor character of the surface need not worry them.

Centre Pompidou, Paris (twentieth century): Architects, Renzo Piano and Richard Rogers

The building's aspirations towards a flexible and media-driven world exist for the connoisseur. The most popular aspects are its 'climbability', by way of the escalator route that dangles over the public side of and offers a three-dimensional extension to the Place Beaubourg, the accessibility of the Centre Pompidou makes it a revealed rather than concealed place of culture, from which one can look down into the Place below. As a simple extension of a favourite icon of the child's world – the climbing frame – the Centre Pompidou is inevitably a popular element in a large city.

Sydney Opera House (twentieth century): Architect, Jørn Utzon

Despite the distortion of Utzon's original internal architecture by small-minded politicians, the proposition remains audacious and the external reality magnificent. Sydney's coastal profile is exotic and the building sits on the end of an existing promontory. As with the Taj Mahal, the key sculptural elements are clear in the mind and sit in unambiguous distinction to the sky, sea and even their base. Yet the latter also seems to be the product of fundamental – even primeval – conditions. It is a continuation of the rocky outcrops of the bay.

In simply describing these six buildings I may well be bypassing those layers and layers of intricacy involved in their building and planning. Similarly, I ignore their subtleties. For it is my purpose here to suggest that public warmth towards a building will be a combination of familiarity and intellectual empathy. The paradox is that many other buildings would be more sustaining if the public could be encouraged to look at them a little longer, or to come inside, wander around and enjoy them. This question of easy recognition has existed between the melody you can whistle and the symphony you can wallow in. Throughout the course of this book I will attempt to interweave examples drawn from all levels of immediacy and try to introduce some fascination for the process of architectural 'delving'.

Curiously, much architectural criticism, and especially that in newspapers, attempts to evaluate buildings from mid-level sighting – afraid to enjoy them as a presence (in the Taj Mahal sense) and unwilling to pursue them as trains of thought. Yet there is a linked architectural culture. Object, complementary object and the experience of the places between them, can all lead to description and evaluation in a simultaneous variety of ways, be it political, technical or experimental.

Different societies have put differing pressures upon their architecture, once we go past superficial tricks, we can sense these pressures. In the United States, the thrust of the pioneers was towards staking-out and then settling, with as many of the key institutions transplanted from Europe as could be rapidly established – the Church (see opposite), the state capital, followed by institutions endowed with grand offices if there was trade, grand silos if there was grain, grand stations if there was traffic. The popularity of the Ecole des Beaux-Arts as a source (and as a finishing-school for architects) was obvious for it could supply the most sophisticated pattern books. Those architects who were sufficiently relaxed, who were regional or who thought directly from first principles were often thought of as threatening to the ideals of civic establishment. It took Frank Lloyd Wright who had created enough of an enigma around his work (coupled with enormous, unstoppable talent) for American architecture to be taken seriously.

In Norway, a peripheral and traditionally 'provincial' role was all that could be expected of a country subordinated to the Danes or the Swedes for so long. Thus, the effects of nationalism in the 1920s was electric. First, a conscious rediscovery of Viking *Jugendstil* mannerisms, then a full-blooded support for social emancipation and social support as a new, classless nation, and consequently, a whole-hearted support for its 'Funkis' or functionalist architecture. Soon this was followed by the realisation of a lifestyle that was unexpectedly high due to cheap timber, electricity and oil and a highly sophisticated and informed architectural community that has worked hard to counterbalance its presumed isolation by developing the most sophisticated and eccentric ideas as well as the mainstream.

Australia is geographically peripheral to an even greater extent. Its hardly benevolent colonial past was hard and basic. Yet out of its comes a remarkable vernacular which more recent architects have recognised as the 'tin' buildings of the outback. The combination of the farm building aesthetic and a carefree psychology that lends itself to lightweight and camping-like technology seems an ideal base for Australian architecture. In parallel, there is an inventive tradition married to the witty critical tradition that is in the direct line of 'what the hell' thinking and that keeps architecture lively, at least on the edges of the cities.

In the case of Germany, however, we have a country that not only represents a much more intensive overlay of events than the other three, but still maintains a fierce regionalism that was until recent times manifested by separate states. Moreover, the geography and political history of Germany suggests a series of cultural influences that stretches into the adjoining countries: Catholicism in the south, Protestantism in the north; the 'valley' culture running into Switzerland and Austria; the Hanseatic connections running along the North Sea; the Rhine

Monticello, Thomas Jefferson, Charlottesville, Virginia, 1771-72

Funkis Architecture, Oslo

Local History Museum, South Kempsey, New South Wales, Glenn Murcutt, 1981-83

as a system of commercial and cultural continuity; the existence of forests and forest-based woodworking and craftsmanship in the Black Forest. The power of the individual states began to wane, but its legacy remains in the aspiration for all cities to possess an Opera and a National Museum as well as a national newspaper. The logic and efficacy of national or global industries means that a door detail or a kitchen component – or a building diagram for that matter – will be similar throughout Germany, but these will be folded, somehow, into notions of what an essentially Bavarian or Saxon interpretation should seem to be like. More than in any other country, sophisticated facilities will certainly be provided and therefore style or form will be added as an aggrandisement of these fundamentals.

In these four national examples, I suggest that there is plenty of reference for the observer – the designer – to work with. The hyperconscious (or cynical) designer can go even further to play upon the American relationship towards European values, institutions or culture; to play upon Norway's possession of space and fuel energy; to indulge in Australia's tin building tradition or to redefine 'locality' in the German sense.

Such values and responses are no worse than those which modern responses discovered by other means, of which some have much less sensitivity running behind them. How many buildings are created in order to exploit a commercial opportunity? How often is the architect left to gloss over this intention with some stylistic gambits that are little more than decoys to the main idea? How many proud, large buildings are designed in order to impress, to intimidate, to distance themselves and the function within from the day-to-day world and its humble pursuits? How many buildings are there that owe their extravagance to national or regional pride ('no, *we* have the biggest dome in the North . . . ')? How many buildings perform a genuine social service?

The legacy of the twentieth century could be that we are just beginning to comprehend the idea of the 'sick' building. Not just due to unhealthy air but more complex syndromes whereby certain types of space and certain modes of enclosure are repressive, depressive and irritating. It could be that instructions

House, Jaywick Sands, Essex, c1937

Grundtvig Church, PV Jensen Klint, Copenhagen, 1921-26

Thorwaldsen's Museum, MGB Bindesbøll, Copenhagen, 1839-48

are given in ways which become really intelligent, taking into account the findings of psychologists and therapists, encouraging the use of lateral thinking (for example, not just asking for a fire station, but thinking afresh about a fireman's lifestyle, about the real need for big red fire engines or better helicopters). The writing of briefs needs to be made by those who are prepared to evolve new typologies.

In parallel, the process of filling and refilling the town by making random series of single buildings may be too primitive. We shall consider in Chapter Two the issue of the building in its context. Meanwhile we can ponder the fact that a high percentage of buildings that we know and use were designed to do something else. It is not always fashion that suggests that an old industrial building yields up a better space in which to live than an apartment block, or that an old school makes a good studio. By extension, then, we could be more innovative in designing fluid-activity buildings.

So far I have been moving into the architectural discussion in a rather general way. But as one begins to move inwards, as a participant, one soon realises that other architects (and perhaps you yourself) collect prejudices and allegiances as fast as football fans. Without noticing it, the critical criteria of aptness or enjoyableness are overlaid by the awareness of which group or which period a building came from.

Major Movements

Quickly bypassing caves, primitive huts, forts and cottages, we arrive at a broad group of mannerisms known as 'Classical'. It is not my purpose to describe Classical systems but to recall that if their origins can be found in Egypt or Assyria, they are most easily defined by looking at the stone buildings of ancient Greece, developed and ornamented by the Romans and associated with their immense exercise of initiative and power. After a respite of several centuries, the trappings of power and the same aesthetics were resurrected in the various stages of Renaissance architecture and culture. Neoclassicism spanned a variety of moods through the Baroque to manufactured and transportable Classicism, which in the nineteenth century could be bolted together from manufactured components.

Every city in every country has plenty of examples of 'Power Classicism'; rather like power-dressing or power-conversation, it is there to impress. One could even say that certain forms of government and certain modes of education feel more comfortable in a Classical building because the hierarchies are stated, the rules are clear. We only have to look at the preferred styles of Hitler, Stalin or Ceausescu for confirmation. If the corollary is some type of woolly, soft escapist architecture, writing from an English background makes the issue piquant. We have a tradition of the picturesque which may involve ruralism, escapism and preferred borrowings from the Gothic, the Chinese or any other (preferably exotic) moment. In a contemporary sense, we can begin to see a link between the personalised world of the walkman, the personal computer and the virtual reality set-up and a history of escape. If we can so easily escape reality *within* reality we are surely sympathetic to the idea of architecture itself having this capability. In the nineteenth century those prefabricated pieces of Classicism could just as easily have been Gothic or Egyptian.

The more you listen to architects discussing their work and that of others, the more you sense a series of positions that will be the product of all this plus a division of opinion between the 'cool' and the 'fruity'; between the rational and the romantic. Yet most suspect of all will be he or she who oscillates between the two, making a highly rational building (in terms of use) in a series of exotic mannerisms. Itsuko Hasegawa's Shonandai Centre, near Tokyo, is a telling example. Her ingenuity and technical wit serves only to irritate the prejudices further, especially since she has also built a number of 'cool' buildings.

In the past it was the Church (or the Moguls or the Shoguns) who had sufficient power to create edifices that could visually dominate a town. Even in modern Poland, quite poor communities have such faith in the Church that they are willing to sacrifice day-to-day facilities to enable the construction of a new and embellished church in their village, the exquisite trappings of which perhaps contrast with the modest scenery surrounding it.

The association of the Gothic with the Church is too far lost in time but somehow it is not enough for us to explain it away by historical logic. It is not just a question of timing but also of form, for example, the stalactite/stalagmite quality of some Gothic forms, the almost monster-like shapes. Awe and 'spookiness' run close together. In the twentieth century we have been confronted by an extraordinary paradox which falls within the field of environment (if you include the experiential). The cinema of the 1930s and later, television, have combined 'glamour' and 'spookiness'. Alongside has been the potential of the electric and the electronic which interweaves the 'there' and the 'not there'. The searchlights of the Nuremberg Rallies and the neon city of night-time Las Vegas disappear at the flick of a switch. The horror movie melts itself into a romance. The hair stands on end; the dream recalls. We have almost bypassed architecture, a state of affairs the cathedral builders could hardly have competed with. But for the moment, the tangible dominates, if only by quantity and familiarity, although

Shonandai Cultural Centre, Itsuko Hasegawa, 1991

House, Wembley Park, London, c 1937

perhaps also by our need to belong. For it is harder to belong to something that disappears at the flick of a switch.

In the past, the presence of the castle and its forces within was a reassurance. Later, the solidity of the corner bank, with its Doric columns was something akin. More recently, you could still walk down a couple of blocks or drive down a highway and reach a high street or a strip that reminded you of the apparatus of support. Shops, facility buildings, public buildings and the like are icons of support. The architect has to remember this and eradicate its symbolism only with the greatest understanding of human psychology. Nonchalance is a difficult design tool.

Modernism of the 1920s or l990s type is far from nonchalant. Its origins were those of a battle for values and for a clean, new world. It adopted a style that had the *a-priori* obligation to strip away the symbols of decadence and tiredness. But now the clarity of purpose and even totality of 1920s Modernism is in danger of being lost in the wake of a Modern revival. Its character has become coded as a style and the parts have become absorbed into an endless repository of form. One of the tasks of the designer is to be clear in the way he uses this repository. It may be that eclecticism is valid, part of a relaxed attitude, part of an open view of culture. Yet the words of Adolf Loos still have a nagging relevance:

> Today ornament on things that have evolved away from the need to be ornamented represents wasted labour and ruined material . . . the artist has always stood at the forefront of mankind full of vigour and health. But the modern ornamentalist is a straggler or pathological phenomenon. He himself will repudiate his own products three years later . . . Freedom from ornament is a sign of spiritual strength. Modern man uses the ornaments of earlier or alien cultures as he sees fit. He concentrates his own inventiveness on other things . (*Ornament Is Crime*, 1908)

In recent years there has been a reintegration of architecture and structural engineering. An architect such as Santiago Calatrava is himself a crossbreed and any definition of which part of his designs is generated from one or other 'direction' becomes completely irrelevant. In the work of Richard Rogers, Norman Foster

Financial Times *Printing Works,*
Nicholas Grimshaw, London, 1988
(detail)

Hotel and Convention Centre, Office for
Metropolitan Architecture, Agadir, 1990

or Nicholas Grimshaw, the structural engineering is integral, not only physically but creatively and intentionally. In this sense there is some continuity of basic Modernism that survives. Yet the observer of architecture – the user of buildings – can be bewildered by all this partisanship. The cut and thrust of historical or non-historical manners matters little if the building doesn't work, or if it irritates profoundly. More subtly, he or she may wish for something to 'grip onto' - some immediately recognised message or code. Classicism provided this more easily than any other style. The calm logic of the column, capital, cornice and base instinctively make sense. Modernism too presented an unequivocal face; an aperture for a window or door. A calm horizontal line for the top. A clear, unadorned face for a wall. You get what you see. As a designer of buildings you are dealing with language and communication. In the process, you are dealing with issues of clarity, nuance, articulation, poetry, irony, literacy, grammar and the rest.

It is just possible that architecture as a language could get lost. It could get submerged in a cybernetic and digitised bank of marginal memory (the initiative for enclosure-making having been taken over by other disciplines using quantified optimal solutions to building problems). The optimum three-person flat, the optimum hundred square metre shop, the optimum six metre workspace; additional visual or referential stimuli being available as a virtual-reality 'service'. Perhaps an add-on element?

From this position, any of the available types of architecture that are based on fabric, structure, or things that you can feel and manipulate, is part of the vernacular. In that case, any efforts that we make to draw together a view of architecture as a whole to see it as a continuous and interrelated sequence of efforts and methods, is a part of tradition. The role of the avant-garde thus becomes merely another element of this continuum.

The Relationship Between 'Regular' and 'High Art' Buildings
As we begin to discriminate between the intriguing and the crass, as we progressively collect more and more examples of design that face several issues at once, and as we begin to recognise more and more nuances, we realise that a whole part of our surrounding world is not engaged in these issues. We start to seek out that part that is engaged, and begin to notice the buildings that offer a sophistication of references. We start to look for nuances. We realise, furthermore, that certain architects are as obsessed by language as they are by form or operation.

Differences of aim have been created by the politics of recognition and criticism. Certainly since the nineteenth century, certain categories of structure have been safely ignored or have fallen into a territory outside normal aesthetic discussion. Industrial plants, temporary objects, workers' cottages and the like seemed to make no contribution to refined culture. By the middle of the twentieth century, however, this had changed. In moving backwards and forwards over the moralities and amusements of design, a creative critic such as Reyner Banham could make a deliberate point of calling our attention to cheap cafes, cars, street items and ephemera of all types. This constant backwards-and-forwards movement of architecture between 'high' and 'low' culture has become one of the fascinations of our time. It is almost as if the designer must not only choose his or her ground for action, but the ground for recognition at the same time.

The advance of architecture as a discipline within universities, or as a referential system has been long and fractious. The difficulty of establishing verifiable criteria may be its charm (for this author and his friends) but also an irritation for the academically inclined. Its discussion is pitched somewhere between art criticism and practical issues. Its aesthetics are not always related to anything measurable or culturally specific.

More recently, especially in the United States, a conscious incorporation of visual codes into the surface of a building has become an elite pastime. Certain architects form a simultaneous academic and linguistic elite that is only concerned with whether or not the resulting buildings function efficiently or communicate with the public at large as long as they amuse and stimulate discussion. Yet we can see from history, that arcane conditions degenerate sooner or later into a moment when those with power will step aside and return to basics, or what they believe to be basics. The simple code whereby big means powerful; classic means ordered; decorative means friendly. This is the type of one-liner architecture with which we started the conversation.

Subsequent chapters therefore have a task: to both amplify the story and unravel the vagaries; to bring forth the issues, experiences and criteria of architecture. Thus, each of us can develop our own points of recognition. Each of us becomes our own observers, our own critic.

Street toilet, Amsterdam ('Not Considered Architecture')

La Villette Pavillion, Bernard Tschumi ('Culturally Loaded Architecture')

House in the clouds, Thorpeness, Essex ('Silly Architecture')

ARCHITECTURE IN CONTEXT

The First Image of the Building

The idea of habit and reward is familiar or us; dog and bone, child and sweet, the award of medals. Such an association can be built up by architecture. The nervous interviewee, for example, is further daunted by the longest ever climb up the steps under the highest ever portal and into the most impressive of marble halls as he proceeds, shaking, towards the interview room.

It has not always been physically necessary for the seat of power to be defendable, yet late castles retained their high walls and crenellations long after anybody was around to attack them. The role, power and mystique of the Church suggested automatically that the edifice must reach up into the sky. As society developed, with increasing complexities surrounding relative power and influence and with the invention of more and more institutions, the ground shifted although not as subtly as one might expect. As most towns expanded, you could still identify significance by a mixture of size, complexity of the main facade and the expense of material. In some cases, there can be the deliberate use of a non-local style. If, for instance, the town consists predominantly of buildings made from the local brick, the stone building will automatically have status. As most towns have used the street system in order to survive, the facing of the street has become the key statement; the dangling of the bone with the implications of the sweet. All too often, the provision of the best internal facilities will have been sacrificed to create an impressive facade.

Twentieth-century architecture has not entirely escaped from this system, though it is a tenet of Modernism that the whole building should be integral and thus all substance of the same quality and consistency. The commercial pressure (plus plenty of hangover of the more primitive wish to show power) has in most cases led to a retreat from this purity. A challenge to this principle of assertion and announcement developed with the Renaissance city, where a single owner or developer would create a total ensemble of street or even a more complex composition involving vistas, squares and circuses.

The role of announcement automatically became more subtle and dependent upon a 'play' between the assumed role of the particular building and the general.

In most cases this is resolved by the fact that the majority of the components were houses where the occupant accepted a degree of anonymity in return for association with the status of the total building. In such architecture one then has to search for clues. The placement of a pediment may not announce anything at all except that this is the centre of a long run of terracing. A considerable familiarity with the architecture may be needed in order to discern the existence of the palace where you learn, eat, pray or feed your horse. With the nineteenth century, however, a return to Romanticism seemed to demand something more, even of urban developments. Towers and turrets began to be used to articulate the ends of streets and a deliberate insertion of a Gothic building into an otherwise neoclassical district would be seen as legitimate articulation.

An intriguing example of such street articulation occurs in Gothenburg where the geometrical shifts of the old canal system act as a base for rebuilding that took place around the turn of the nineteenth and twentieth centuries. A variety of newer, taller buildings was then inserted and at the end of every straight run there is a turret. Because of the geometry of the canals, the next run of buildings is out of sight, but you are beckoned onwards by the turret and you will come upon them after the corner. Such a device also works well in silhouette, suiting the light conditions of the North. The individual buildings are quite distinct, but the articulation of the city encompasses both a 'civic' obligation and an aesthetic of the 'particular'.

Such a town, being both established and industrialised by the end of the nineteenth century, contains many buildings that incorporate the explosion of mechanical technique and variety of materials which could send signals to the onlooker. Extra detail could be cast in iron and pressed out in terracotta; ornament was infinitely applicable; materials could be imported from anywhere; mannerisms of style could be overlaid and combined. Such a situation has continued until today but the skilful designer has to recognise the progressive tendency towards the symbolism of materials and manufactured details. The use of plate glass, mosaic or stone almost certainly makes a statement of status. In certain conditions stainless steel, glass blocks and marble will make parallel statements. The question

Liver Building, Liverpool, 1908-10

Town Museum, Elmshorn, nineteenth century

of what is appropriate therefore becomes a socio-political issue as much as it might be to do with construction or function.

Meanwhile, there had been a period where an international code existed involving style – Classical for government, Gothic for the Church, Roman for banks, extended vernacular for schools. Surely the exceptions are equal in number, but the code is instantly recognisable to the uninitiated passer-by. The new architecture of the 1930s and afterwards – broadly categorised as Modernism or the International Style – attacked this on all fronts. It attacked the use of ornament, archaic symbolism and any kind of fake. The Arts and Crafts Movement in England and the *Werkbunds* of Germany and Austria sought a return to the 'honesty' of direct craftsmanship and construction which did not always lead to the 'Modernist' aesthetic, but similarly challenged the 'applied' symbols. Our cities, which are predominantly the creation of the 1960s onward, are filled with architecture that is caught in various hybrid combinations of both Modernist cleansing and the return to popular symbolism.

Brilliant models of a direct architecture do exist where the culture, and surroundings, its spirit and resources, can be contrived into an identifiable place. The housing of port workers in Amsterdam by Willem de Klerk (and later Ferdinand Kramer) took advantage of the highly developed brick-building techniques of that city and then evolved a series of ingenious parts that unashamedly celebrate the entering of a doorway, the ventilation of a kitchen, the waiting inside a post-office, the turning of a corner; in other words, making the architecture out of the commonplace events of a modest community.

Thus we can see two fundamental approaches to the issue of architecture in context; the first consisting of 'marker' buildings that are totally self-absorbed, the second of a shared language for all buildings. In parallel, we can see two moralities of symbolic form. The first is concerned with the familiar, the referential (and thus most probably, populist intentions); the second, with the integrity of the discipline of architecture itself (thus physically and intellectually tougher and harder for the layman to understand). In all cases, the primary features of the building may or may not be discrete. It is possible to create a 'decoy' facade,

Jarrolds Works, John Brown and Richard Parkinson, Norwich, 1834

Warehouses, Hamburg, nineteenth century

Spaarndammerburt Housing, Block 2, Michel de Klerk, Amsterdam, 1915-17

or for the frontal character to be calculated as a screen or a mask which is there expressly to communicate with the street. Again, architectural moralities on the twentieth century have encouraged the idea that the external architecture is the internal architecture: a state of total integrity with exposure of the workings and atmosphere of the internal scenery. This runs parallel to late twentieth-century moralities regarding the social obligations of the Institution or the Facility. We can measure the degree to which it is necessary to enter the building in order to read or experience it, and such a motive can be established at the very early stages of a design, remaining a central issue of the pitch of the work.

Our recognition of the role of the building can involve basic questions. Is it an 'open' or 'shut', 'public' or 'private' object? Is it a 'full frontal' edifice or does it withdraw from public confrontation? Is it 'elemental' or 'encased'? Is it obviously conscious of other models of its type, or an independent piece of work? From this list of questions, we can discern another layer of presentation that is involved regarding the components themselves. The internal elements may have greater levels of articulation than the outer face. A building may be well mannered towards the street and allow it to 'all hang out' at the back or towards the courtyard in the case of European 'block' buildings. The subtleties of detail that proclaim 'publicness' are complex. In the late twentieth century, sheer scale may not be sufficient, nor scale of detail. Complexity of detail can as often indicate cheapness, crassness or lack of sophistication as the reverse. The private apartment block is not necessarily devoid of those very same instincts that we met in the traditional seats of power. Similarly, the references to other buildings of the same purpose are now overlaid by issues of international brand image. The gas station, supermarket or hotel will seek to remind us of its almost universal presence (and therefore quality or power). This is easy, but without the big sign we have to observe the architectural *parti* that is probably only quasi-functional.

The Role of the Building in the Town

We have already referred to the early elements of a community, but the designer has to spend much time understanding the role of a building at two levels: first,

Apartment House, Oslo, c1910

'Z' Bank, Günther Domenig, Vienna, 1979

its functional intricacies and their reciprocal roles, and then the external demonstration that we wish for them. Moreover, any analysis of the last hundred years will expose the enormous shift between the function originally intended for many buildings and their present day function. This is as it should be. Intelligent design must involve both prediction for change, provision for adaptation and provision for the exchange of parts of the building.

A condemnation of the nineteenth and twentieth-century suburb has often revolved around its monotony or its endlessness, yet in a small old town there is a 'collage' of types, where all is rapidly visible. Insertions of the 'untypical' can, as we have seen, be banal but they remain a necessity in the face of unimaginative urban development. The English pub at the crossroads, the diner on the American strip; both have lead to a twenty-first-century model of useful incident with its own typology. How does a community accept or reject the built insertion? Must the aesthetic be in tune and in period with that of the surrounding buildings? Once again, the small old town offers a clue; by definition the whole place is a collage of style-jumps and time-jumps in close proximity and we accept its charm. If possible, it seems that the inserted object should first of all have its own integrity; secondly, it should try to articulate this both inside and out, and then make such allowances of 'good manners' that do not interfere with the rest, but equally do not fall into false mimicry. Our civilisation also deserves more than a few beacons of progress.

We can recall memorable streets where the theatre of incident and counterpoint might have very parallel features to that of well-composed music, involving interval, accentuation, repetition, tonal quality and crescendo. The contributory parts may appear to be successful in picturesque circumstances. The question is how to assess the role demanded of the new insertion? The street strip needs to be drawn, the map of figure-and-ground recognised, the nuance of the aforementioned 'musical' balance analysed. Can there be a dialogue with the street? Can a building assess its role in relation to the adjoining plaza, garden, street corner, alley, courtyard or other evacuated space? The play between the solid object and nearby evacuated spaces is a key to the question of both identity

Typical British suburban end wall, c1935

American diner, Roppongi, Tokyo, c1990

and articulation. In the house designed for a physician at La Plata, near Buenos Aires, Le Corbusier used a very small and proscribed site as a layered series of elements, developing the 'screen' element from the street to create a proscenium arch leading on to a very small courtyard with a single tree. Ramps lead up to the building proper as a layered background. The parts are exposed, but only at close quarters, and the levels are contributory – as is the tightness of the basic condition to a spatial and theatrical pocket that also contribute to the street.

In certain circumstances, the identity of the building can be the reverse of an absorbed condition. There may be a vista, a sight-line or a path that causes the internal arrangement to focus towards it; a major window, a balcony or doorway that lines up and responds from within. The result can be idiosyncratic and there may be a conscious development of the topmost parts. I have already referred to the expressionistic value of the skyline in dark weather; other incentives also exist such as the giving of identity in the face of optimal plans creating optimal facades.

It has sometimes been possible to coerce a series of independent buildings into a degree of commonality or reciprocity that present to the city an *ensemble*. It can be magnificent. In history it has happened by virtue of geography or land values: 'Downtown' and 'Midtown' Manhattan are outcrops from the heroic scale of the whole; Stockholm's islands present a conveniently scaled series of urban clusters; Sydney Harbour narrows towards the downtown (with the unique coupling of the Bridge and the Opera House articulating an already iconographic situation).

The sensitive designer will search for lines of definition, markers, things to respond to, spaces to extend from, views to tantalise in order hopefully to achieve this at an appropriate scale. The success of Carlo Scarpa as a miniaturist cannot conceal the general dangers of fussiness.

Local Context and Local Conditions

It is ironic that so many architects have attempted to transfer mannerisms from their point of origin to alien territory, often with inappropriate materials and unlikely climate. One looks hard for the ways in which the admirer of the Classical Greek style will deal with a condition where there is a relative lack of shadow.

Doctor's villa, Le Corbusier, La Plata, near Buenos Aires, 1949

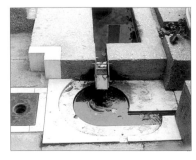

Querini–Stampalia Foundation, Carlo Scarpa, Venice, 1973 (detail)

Exploration of indigenous techniques often 'cuts off' as soon as the familiar model seems to be achievable. The local brick may not be *travertine*, but it can be plastered and painted to look well enough like it, hence the now much admired 'stucco' of London, Brighton and Bath. The transfer of Classicism to New England eventually encountered such a degree of circumstantial logic offered by the proliferation of timber that it was willing to adapt and, in many senses, refine its details.

The particular stripped-down 'flavour' of late Swedish or Danish Classicism is readable as both a local and a sophisticated architectural style. Australian 'tin' buildings of the late twentieth century look to be moving towards a similar status. The reduced profiling and calm elementalism combined with bravura plan geometry that can be found in recent Catalan architecture is a further example. In all these cases, the architecture is highly developed, very conscious and refined. The architects concerned were literate and aware of other traditions and mannerisms and were certainly aware of Greek origins (in the case of the Swedes), European and American technologies (in the case of the Australians) and both Italian Rationalism and Scandinavian Functionalism (in the case of the Catalans). In these instances, Regionalism is neither modest, populist nor traditional. It is nonetheless, distinctive.

Arguably, the most architectonically dynamic cities are those in which activity abounded; be it manufacture, traffic, trade and invention. Cities such as Barcelona, Chicago, Glasgow, Tokyo, Milan and Antwerp have a high incidence of architectural initiative. One finds that original and inventive architecture was more acceptable in such cities. All over town there have been people designing and contriving, with architecture being merely one 'wing' of this general activity. Predominantly 'governmental' cities have tended to be more conservative and pompous – as would be expected. Ports are intriguing, partly because of the existence of the ships which are forms of architecture in themselves, and because of the influx of people, materials and ideas from elsewhere. All of them need districts in which the bourgeoisie can escape the smells and inconveniences of industry or railway; all of them need services; all of them create districts of activity, commerce or pleasure. Once again, the individual building can either thrive on its location within the system, hide from it or pretend that it is somewhere else. Hence the *palazzo* that enjoys being close to the market place, the railway station that would like to be a palace (with the illusion shattered by the give-away sound of the train) the enigmatic blank wall with the small door that leads into a delightful hidden courtyard or, in another direction altogether, the high-rise office building that not only sits with its first operational floor some eight metres above ground, but with every sinew of its tinted glass set to detach itself from the local *milieu*. The designer has to decide upon the degree of involvement that must be created between the building and the community. If the answer is 'very little', the mannerisms will need to be very assured, the payoff worth the detachment.

There have been cases where the architectural *milieu* itself has created the mystique of a local mannerism around the reputation of an honoured architect, with Mackintosh as the reference in Glasgow, Egon Eirmann imitated by his many ex-students in Karlsruhe and the houses of Maybeck revered in San Francisco. A highly sophisticated set of parts can be used by quite modest designers and the paradox lies in the question as to whether reference or escape is more valid. Any architect working in such a place is made well aware that these deities exist!

Foibles

The discussion of context has so far revolved around the town and the city where confrontation is more immediate. In other circumstances, however, there can be just as exacting conditions of confrontation. The idea of a gentle, totally absorbing landscape is a romantic dream since the practical demands of farming and the directness in terms of techniques and resources are often tough. In many places, the indigenous material – the local stone or timber – gives not only 'character' to the constructed building but, more simply, *is* the building. Aesthetically, the building may well become a mere incident in the composition created by husbandry, sheltering, enclosure – these in the broad, open sense of fields, hedges, yards, and lines of trees. A favourite concept of my own is the notion of the highly engineered (even manufactured) architectonic object peeping out through a gap in the hedge. The components used in farm buildings have become an increasingly used resource by architects such as Stanley Saitowitz (especially his early work in the Transvaal) and Glenn Murcutt in New South Wales. The context of isolation seems to clear the mind, making the interweaving of veneers of surface more than usually ridiculous.

More problematic is the increasingly pressured territory sometimes referred to as the 'edge' – an internationally familiar zone that is neither as identifiable as a 'suburb' nor as tranquil or localised as the true countryside. Often related to the road network and the proximity (but not presence) of a major zone of population, the buildings within have many of the same reciprocal roles of the early days of town-making. There cannot be too many of the same type (lest they cancel each other out commercially), yet there needs to be just enough to act reciprocally (the supermarket vis-à-vis the home-care shed vis-à-vis the car

Johnson's Warehouse, Ivar Tengbom, Stockholm, 1922

Farmhouse, Glenn Murcutt, Mount Irvine New South Wales, 1977-80

Brebnor House, Stanley Saitowitz, Schoemansville, Transvaal, 1976

showroom). The fundamental enclosures are similar; sophisticated sheds with an almost graphic design approach to expression, and which can no doubt be easily replaced and refitted. Along with the hotel lodges and out-of-town offices they could establish a focus to the 'edge', but so far lack definition as objects. One is reminded of the establishment of the American 'strip' in an earlier generation which is equally interchangeable but often more integral with a nearby community.

Architects could offer more to the genre. Though not considered worthy of consideration in schools of architecture, the typology is ready to be developed intelligently and inventively. The noncommittal nature of their condition need not be a deterrent to their development. Similarly, with the many non-contextual or non-urban installations such as yards, industrial lots, warehousing and production sheds, they have no less intrinsic potential than the old department stores and brick warehouses that we now try to preserve. Instead of wrapping a paper-thin graphic skin onto the public face, we can consider the wrapping round and over of functioning cells of buildings.

Urbane qualities are valued. The identification of these in the language of individual buildings would be a summary of the last few pages, and their identification in the composite form of a district should be clear. However, we are in danger of losing our technique for creating the town. The nineteenth century left a heritage of both heroism and subtlety in its development of role-playing types – the hotel, the arcade, the terrace, the station, the public baths, the public library, the department store, the winter garden – where climate and shelter, as well as casual display, were permitted or even celebrated. Currently we employ the mall, the corner precinct and the hotel lobby as extensions of this tradition.

To weave amongst the remnants of the city, seen as a balanced set of elements against the settled suburb and the wayward 'edge', is to play a game where the stakes are high. 'Downtown' revival is already an established issue, corporate image versus the locality is also familiar, while more than ever before, the 'unseen' network of outer suburbia and the 'edge' demands a softer approach, with new typologies that may never return to total, formalised structures. As for contextual pressures, they become fragmented into an endless variety of response.

Toy Store, Venice, California, c1990

Arcade, Rue des Petits Champs, Paris 1824

Eaton Centre, Eberhard Zeidler, Toronto, 1973-81

25

BUILDINGS AS COMMON SENSE

Buildings as Containers

The castle can be observed as an early container for large numbers of people. All that was necessary fundamentally was a good wall and adequate supplies. Immediately one has the programme of first, the fundamental container, and secondly, that which sustains the contained people. Curiously, the equation fits so many other types: the theatre contains the audience and the stage sustains them; the arena contains the crowd and the game on the pitch sustains them; the ship transports the people and the engine room sustains them. Critical is the appropriateness, and probably the simplicity, of that relationship. Of next importance, as far as the crowd is concerned, is the interface with the world outside. Those being sustained – soldiers, musicians or whoever – may be related more discretely to that world. The crowd tends to celebrate its presence in the large room. Hence the significance of the foyer, the vestibule, the cafeteria, the bar. Indeed, the more bourgeois the public and leisurely the event, the more this foyer space becomes a conceptual parallel theatre to the formal one.

These three conditions understood and met, there remains a tantalising territory for the designer to deal with, namely, the stringing-together of the parts of the large room with the foyer and with the world outside. Elsewhere in the building there is a parallel issue, often more modestly designed; the sustaining of the stage (in the case of the theatre). A decision may be made either to wrap all the parts into a single box and thus lose the linking elements as well as the secondary main room into the overall shape; it might be to articulate the two or three main elements; or it might be to demonstrate externally the linkages as well. This last option is almost always formally evocative.

So far I have mentioned nothing about shape. This is quite intentional. Even though arena buildings are often distinctive as shapes and many architects crave to exploit any usable characteristics of the main generating diagram, it seems absolutely necessary to understand the principal spaces; first of all, to clarify the behaviour expected within them and of them as spaces, then to clarify the mode of exchange between them. Only at the end of the process can the envelope be coerced into some particular shape.

Tokyo Zoo Monorail, 1955

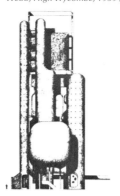

Furniture Manufacturers' Association Headquarters, Michael Webb, High Wycombe, 1959 (project)

Nonetheless, there is a certain power to the idea of several hundreds or more people moving in a predictable direction over a short time, and this power can be interpreted in the forceful positioning of the surrounding walls. There can be a certain scale of incident in the public spaces which does not have to be reflected in the hidden or subordinate spaces. It is as if there is a body with its mouth, stomach and lungs surrounded by necessary flesh. Unfortunately, the analogy breaks down at one critical stage. The substance of buildings does not include the element of the muscle, not in the sense of a flexing and dynamically responding piece of substance. Therefore, all those conditions that come under pressure – valves, junctions, meeting-points – have to be designed intelligently. As often as not, they will be over-scaled in order to take on the most pressured moments.

History has evolved a two-way traffic that celebrates both the idea of the 'public' stomach of large buildings and the 'muscle substitutes'. There is usually a *largesse* of scale, with large doors, high ceilings and a predilection for bringing in windows at high level and probable lighting of the ceiling of the largest spaces. There is particular celebration of the 'valves', whether by consciously making them places at which to slow down and ponder, or in the pursuit of articulate format, making them subject to special conditions of lighting, surfacing or perhaps, in exotic cases, the celebratory placement of domes.

Before moving down scale, the designer of exhibition halls, auditoria or other gathering-places should take advantage of the true legacy of the twentieth century: transportation and war. Consider the ways in which large ships take advantage of both the internal focus and the external view, percolating the edges of large rooms with decks, balconies and diagonal connections. Consider also the ways in which airports have to keep the movement running forward (but so often get tied up in the necessity to change level at the most irritating moment). The aircraft carrier is another beautiful object to study, with its long deck pre-eminent, literally overriding all else except for the thin sliver of superstructure. This same deck is then provided with 'mouths' in the form of palettes which can descend (with their captive 'plane) down into the substructure. In this case, there is certainly a moment of muscle!

As soon as we are dealing with particular sets of people, the language and definition of space – its hierarchical interpretation and its articulation – seem to become much easier. The way we walk may be a first clue; differently in church from in an airport, differently in a supermarket from in a school. Extremely influenced by this, we might be expected to round the corners of one and set gleaming columns at the corners of another. We might be expected to cover the floors of one with gravel and the other with sleek rubber flooring. Yet we seem to adhere to a middle territory of well-behaved right-angled corners and similarly orthodox surfaces. I am not sure whether this is appropriate. It could be that architects are still too wedded to the 'neatness' principle, whereby the crisp corner and predictable surface are said to be reassuring (or maybe, just easy). Observation of the street and of wear and tear – though not usually thought of as a reference-ground for architects – could offer clues of a much more inventive series of artefacts created in the wake of simply going round the corner.

Much will depend upon our understanding of the activities within, for example, the way in which these activities balance out, along with considerations of size, intensity, equipment, light requirement and noise conditions. In parallel, much will depend upon our assessment of the habits and rituals that have grown up in the tradition of the building type. There have been broad social movements that have affected the form of architecture: tendencies that span across functional demands. In industrial developments, the agglomeration of series of structures in which each was tailor-made for the process or machinery within, has been replaced progressively by the creation of simple 'shed' structures in which the various processes can be housed under a general condition of lighting and servicing, with the attitude that the residual 'slack' or even 'wasted' space is cheaper and more simple to enclose than the joining together of separate structures. Moreover, the processes and machinery may be changed at any time, so extra space will be needed. Department stores, warehouses and supermarkets have followed this principle but it has been resisted by some otherwise highly functional types such as hospitals and schools where the envelope is still the product of the agreed 'social' or 'operational' group. The reasons are clear: in such buildings,

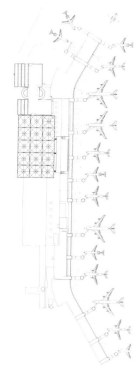

Marseille Airport, Richard Rogers, 1994

Stansted Airport, Norman Foster, 1991, (entrance from railway)

Eurostar Terminal, Nicholas Grimshaw, Waterloo Station, London, 1994

28

the well-being of the people themselves is paramount and contact with the window is psychologically important. In parallel, however, is the significance of the organised 'group' to the institutions (in these cases, the ward or the class and formal expression, which can sometimes be seen as the registration of this organisation more than anything else).

Office buildings and hotels are caught in a midway point, whilst the need for identity and view vis-à-vis the window has now been reaffirmed. Following some periods of mid-twentieth-century experiment, there has not been the same incentive to compartmentalise. The part of a floor that can be served by a fire escape is defined in virtually all countries and the number of bedrooms served by a hotel linen room is also fairly universal. But these have only operational significance and can only be traced as parts of multiples; for example, an office floor of three escapes, or a hotel floor of two linen rooms. Thus, the equations begin to pan out with a certain 'endlessness'. The social critic can comment that in factories, supermarkets, offices and hotels the commercial payback is paramount, whereas hospitals and schools still have a deep-rooted social and humanitarian role. Our response to this as designers can then take one of two directions, either to accept the definition and use the differences of 'endlessness' or 'compartmentalisation' as the first design parameter. Alternatively, we can treat our design as a piece of social rhetoric which coerces conditions of 'locality' or 'identity' towards parts of the endless mass. It depends upon a political view, but also upon the value that you place upon expressionism. Take, for example, a lump of building bulging-out, saying 'hello' as it were. What is its significance? Is it not common sense to make a bedroom window quite standard, along with two hundred others on the same wall? Is any despair at the mass of two hundred identical items a mere piece of sensitivity inherited from a village mentality?

Where the purpose of the building is itself complex and where there is a tradition of particularity, we are on more simple moral ground, but with far more options. We have to know the processes and mythologies to an even greater extent. In the case of a museum we have to understand the academic plot of the curators. In the case of a restaurant we have to understand the

City Bank lobby, Omaha, c1905

Offices and restaurant, Sundahl and Thunström, 1935

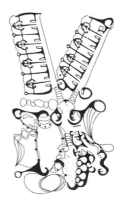

The Smiling Lion Hotel – Lourenço Marques, Amancio Guedes, Mozambique, 1956-58, (project)

theatrical plot, in the case of a library we have to weigh up the aspects of it as both a sanctuary and as a machine for information retrieval (which will anyhow – as in the case of the museum – depend upon the academic plot). In this category, the sheer volume or speed of the users is less dramatic than in the stadium or theatre. However, something far more subtle has to be accommodated, once again making demands upon our attitude towards expressionism.

How can patterns of enclosure, or even extended form, really respond to the state of mind of a person standing or sitting in a space? How can it really introduce its atmosphere and layers of value to the passer-by? I have deliberately avoided any discussion of geometry in this chapter. Much architecture is based upon geometrical habit (almost all rectilinear – it's so sensible, isn't it?). Other architecture is based upon games of geometry enjoyed by the designer. Once embarked upon triangulation, rolling round a curve or the sport of homing-in onto 'node' points, the design process is actually a mixture of observing the issues of action, function and inherent myth (that I have described so far), along with that same triangulation, rolling and homing. Retaining a common-sense attitude to design is difficult enough in the face of socio-politico-commercial instincts, but even more so when one begins to get a taste for the delight with which an elegant curve can progressively open out the vista towards the sea, or the octagonal enclosure giving rise so happily to the glass pinnacle above. Thus, we are caught in a three or four-way game.

At the most personal level, the enclosing wall and its release through a window puts as great a pressure upon the sensitivity and the logic of a designer as any large piece of planning. On the part of the user, irritations are immediate. On the part of the architect, there is little room for manoeuvre. Neither the idea of 'slack' (as in the modern factory) nor the idea of 'progressive absorption' of a new space (as in a public building) is likely at close quarters, or in a small building. It is much more as if a secret series of radar waves are being bounced back and forth between the person sitting at the table and the corner of the room, the dark patch of wall, the sudden slit of reflected light, the view through the window, the shimmer of the glass, the echo of activity in the next room –

Guard House, Katsura Imperial Palace, Kyoto, from 1590

'Underground Berlin' Projection Tower, Lebbeus Woods, 1988 (project)

Pyrch House, John and Patricia Patkou, Victoria, British Columbia, 1983

one could extend such a list to the point of tedium. The designer has meanwhile organised the window position well enough. It can even be argued that optimal positioning may be doing the occupant a great disservice. The moral issue of aptness against the 'lowest common denominator' exists in every creative and cultural field – the 'easy' tune, the 'simple' text, the 'realistic' painting and now, the 'obvious' place for the window. We have only to erect some examples of perversity such as rooms with no view, inaccessible corners, or unbearable acoustics to return anxiously to the optimal.

It need not be as tiresome. An elegant example of dealing with several of these issues in a modest space is the house at Victoria, British Columbia by Patricia and John Patkau. The immediate suburban surroundings were banal, so the immediate outside space is a small sunken court. The sight lines of the window allow it to be the periphery of the 'readable' space, but the sky opens up to suggest a further dimension of the world beyond. Meanwhile, the geometry involved is sufficiently intriguing to be particular. Without being too tricky, the actions and possibilities of the inhabitant within are direct generators of a fine example of imaginative design.

Buildings as Machines

A cool look at time-and-motion can suggest a layout, and modern computer technology can certainly produce optimal paths. In the light of this, most of the discussion here will revolve around the mythologies that cause us to prefer that which is not strictly rational.

In recent history, function was invoked as the basis of a philosophical position in architecture. Functionalism suggested that the operational diagram could generate the plan, without over-emphasis and assuming a clarified style of white walls and the simplest of openings. Was this the result of cultural conditioning, or was it psychological? The inability to stay satisfied by this logic lies at the root of our love/hate relationship with irrationality. Most likely an architect will move backwards and forwards in the argument for his building between a 'straight' description of organisational logic and a series of value-added descriptions.

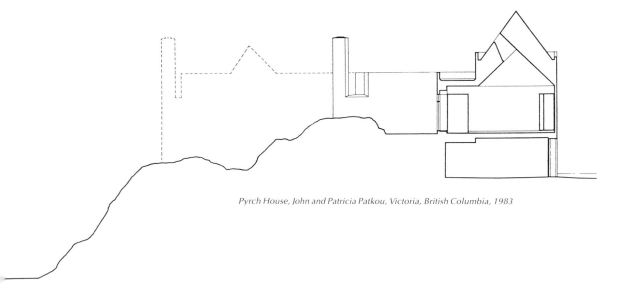

Pyrch House, John and Patricia Patkou, Victoria, British Columbia, 1983

There are a few building types that are satisfied by the creation of the operating diagram. In the case of the 'sub-terminal' to Terminal 1 at London's Heathrow Airport (dealing with flights to Ireland) Nicholas Grimshaw has produced a tailored skin that calls to mind the specificity of an aeroplane itself. The parts are only the size that the operation needs and the diagram is similarly tight and logical. It is an essay in 'direct tailoring'. A completely different level of being involved with a machine is experienced by anyone going to Frank Lloyd Wright's Guggenheim Museum in New York. The building makes a particular demand upon us as we enter: we go up the elevator and then follow our basic instincts in circling down and down (pausing from time to time to look at some art on the walls). This heroic extrapolation of the helter skelter deals with fundamental mechanics. The strength of character of the architecture prevents us from considering the game too silly or too simplistic. In the case of another heroic object of modern architecture, the Van Nelle factory in Rotterdam, the bridges flying at all angles establish the architectural power of machine-as-form. It is a straightforward facility as well as a formal celebration of geometry produced by the machine.

The connoisseur analysing the building-as-machine first looks for those parts where the process starts: the delivery deck of industrial and commercial buildings, the main entrance of public buildings (which will be discussed in the next chapter) and any places where the general 'flesh' of the building has been pared away to reveal the 'guts'. Having identified the core, or spinal system, he will then search for a logic to the fleshing-out. The nature of the flesh itself should be the product of careful consideration of the role played by each room. This is followed by grouping certain rooms together, based upon known functions. There will come a point, however, where the range of room sizes and the juxtaposition of the rooms themselves gives a 'ragged' pattern, if dealt with functionally. At this point, the designer is faced with a paradox; to stick to the analysis, or to start to optimise around the sensible logic of grouping together rooms of a certain size. In other instances, he may put rooms of certain sizes in a typical position vis-á-vis the entrance, or vis-à-vis the core. Dealing with this paradox, one eventually builds up a technique of anticipation of such problems to produce a plan where

Pier 4A, Heathrow Airport, Nicholas Grimshaw, London, 1993

Guggenheim Museum, Frank Lloyd Wright, New York, 1943-69

rooms of particular sizes (and similar roles in the hierarchy and operation of the building) appear to support a clear, balanced and uncomplicated piece of flesh.

The experienced designer is like the general of an army, at all times needing to relate tactics to strategy, to take counter-action to action and to watch his flank. The fact that a building is static, as opposed to a live battle, is deceptive as the use of the building is 'live'. Such action can be observed most clearly in a court of law or an airport, where different streams of people need to be both directed, separated and treated differently. By contrast, it would be a fascinating exercise to make a similar observation of a religious building or any other in which ritual is overlaid by common-sense positioning of walls, doors and sight-lines. In the end, the vexing issue of interpretation can confuse those of us with a mind for the obvious.

Buildings as Shelter or Survival Mechanisms

In the developed countries of northern Europe, we are rarely confronted with extreme challenges to our houses or workplaces. These buildings survive in reasonable fashion and degrees of expected suitability, enabling us to relish the nuances of style and motive, which go far beyond the fundamental issue that they are built for our survival. Most of the time they handle the climate and only require modest repair. As other conditions of climate are encountered, the fundamental reminder begins to appear and at moments of earthquake and flood the reminder is even stronger. Occasionally – and it is rare – someone will call attention to the ridiculous nature of some of our constructional habits or will have the audacity to suggest that the house (as it has developed) may not be the most intelligent form of shelter. In the mid-twentieth century, a few extraordinary designers set up these questions from a position of intellectual puzzlement at the lack of fundamental thinking lying interwoven into our ways of making shelter. Pre-eminent in this was Richard Buckminster Fuller who created a lifetime of questions regarding energy, effort, weight and universality. His 'Dymaxion' domes, homes, cars and structures that could cover a whole city became the most discussed prototype systems in the world. Not only that, but 'Bucky' domes continue to sprout all over what he himself described as 'the Spaceship Earth'. In the course of time, these are mostly used in the more superficial sense of being a sensible, cheap and light form of space-cover, thus bypassing much of his more critical applications of the Dymaxion principle. The idea of a marvellous, self-supporting and lightweight 'package' was almost simultaneously being investigated by Konrad Wachsmann, whose 'Turning Point of Building' became a key point of departure for those architects of the 1960s to 1980s who developed ideas around the idea that technology could return to fundamentals regarding the making and the 'packaging' of buildings. That the sophistication of joints and components could at the same time imply a fundamental simplicity of method and solution might seem a paradox, yet Wachsmann's dream was the 'packaged' house and subsequently the vast structured shelter, of as great beauty as universality.

With the inevitable questioning that came from Victor Papeneck and subsequent 'green' positions, a certain disenchantment set in regarding the technological solutions to survival problems. If the position has now become less polemical, it may well be a result of steady investigation on the part of scientists, engineers and inventors who are continuously emerging with techniques and devices that seem to be neither totally 'technical' nor narrowly 'natural', but simply the result of our steadily increasing ability to measure, test and co-relate phenomena. My unemotional summary on this point is really to remind us that we are looking at things from a common-sense position. So much polemic can arise once the quasi-religious issue of 'survival' and 'technology' is mentioned, yet ignoring the necessary work yet to be done.

Climate has not yet been fully understood, even as combinations of basic principles of shelter, breeze, solar energy or even relationships of structure to earth are still being developed. A further territory exists where traditional principles of warming and cooling are being interwoven with electronic, electrical or machine-based systems of sensing and response, or even where these are being interwoven with the familiar fuel-based techniques. The planning stage of many structures still seems to divide itself into two areas – the first where things are positioned and the second where these positions are made climatically and structurally possible by the insertion of 'techniques' borrowed from any of the philosophical or experiential positions just described. Only in the hottest and coldest countries do we bother to combine the two stages or even organise the comfort and survival issues at the outset. It is fascinating to observe a normally urbane designer such as Ralph Erskine making projects for the Arctic or near-Arctic condition. His naturally exuberant abilities are even further released when he digs into the climatic problems of such a place; the orthodox forms of our cities suddenly have no relevance. The normal restraints of surface are similarly bypassed in the tropical condition of Ken Yeang's Kuala Lumpur house, where the breeze is caught and folded over the Modernist villa, producing the architectural equivalent of a sail plane, or when the normal definitions of 'wall', 'screen', 'roof', 'awning', 'floor' or 'veranda' are stretched and folded into a relaxed language for the modestly warm climate of New South Wales by Richard le Pastria at Cammeray.

The basic principles investigated by these three very different architects do not result in primitivism. Quite the reverse. They are investigations that use invention and combinations of value as well as combinations of technique. The development of architecture has been the product of similar combinations in the past; particularly advantageous in periods less self-conscious than our own. The effects of exposure to sea, wind, water, snow or sand are, in a sense, conducive to creativity. The response is not limited to buildings, for ships and wind breaks have battled and invented. More intriguingly, buildings that are created in proximity to these devices begin to imitate or borrow from them. Some of the best detailing is to be found in shipbuilding cities, and some of the most dramatic architecture is found at the extension of sea walls. Similarly, some of the most straightforward design is found in military defences where the task is direct and basic – to withstand and protect. The analyst's objective should therefore be to identify the main task. And we can see that this may not be a facility but a need. This task may be a circumstance and then, only then, can the ebb and flow of action between the working parts be manipulated.

There is no moral here. Once again, the order of priority takes a matter-of-fact view – depending upon the place and the time – and as a final twist, an invention of all the normal priorities still, quite often, leads to a marvellous building.

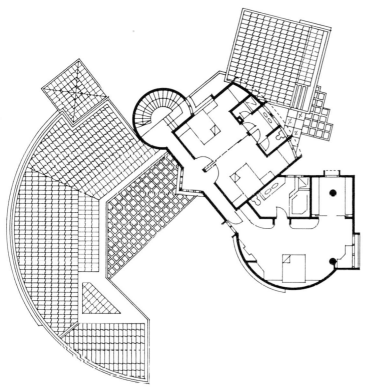

Dason House, Ken Yeang, Kuala Lumpur, 1988

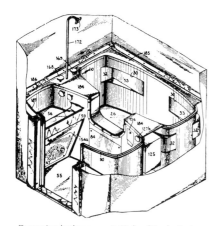

Dymaxion bathroom unit, Richard Buckminster Fuller, 1937

Scout hut, Ralph Erskine, Lovö, near Drottingholm, 1953

35

ENTERING AND IDENTIFYING

Getting Into a Building

Across all varieties of architecture there is an acknowledged magic to the business of entering. It is sustained through the vicissitudes of style, importance, functionality or any other constraint. If the moment of discovery of 'the within' is inherited from the instincts of eating, sex and hunting, it is also to be found in formal behaviour. The momentary pause for the celebration should prepare us for the entrance to be the most heavily invested point on a building.

We see illustrated on pages 38-39, a combination of devices. Some involve the porch or steps, others the secondary issues of climbing up into the building or sheltering before entry. In most examples, the language of the rest of the building is used, having sufficient ingredients for the business of lining the orifice, intensifying the pressure of its incident or detail and, maybe, supporting a pediment or canopy, or disappearing into a porch. Having defined the typical, one can enjoy a fascinating byway that seems to have evolved in Scandinavia in the early twentieth century and that has been sustained through to recent work labelled 'deconstructive'. The entrance is a separate piece or form, with quite disassociated characteristics when seen against the rest of the building. It can sometimes resemble a 'tongue'. It can accost the street. It can become a pavilion in its own right. We can question this whole issue of the building and its 'tongue' by trying to categorise the canvas canopies typical of New York that protect the limousine passengers as they enter their lobbies. The street is for a moment captured but the building remains complete and in control. Airport jetways are a further example of the late twentieth century taking faltering steps towards a building that reaches out. In both cases, the element is a removable extra.

In purist and post-purist architecture, the entrance can be relatively mute, a spatial intervention that does not interrupt the geometry of the wall. In the nineteenth century too, vestibules can be recessed from the street – most often protected by doors or gates but intended to be exposed. These examples are from the city and respond to urban demands. Thus entrances – which are pressure points – can be discussed as reflections of life. The sociology of a church is different from that of a farm; the business of entering a villa is quite different from entering a block of apartments, although they both act as houses.

Most architects are concerned with the opportunity to show off their sophistication at the point of entry, but a moment of thought about the theatre, the psychology and the dynamics of the actual entry could lead to even more architectural ideas. At an extreme point lies the performance of waiting at the entrance to a hotel or theatre. The canopy is part of a sequenced set of wide spaces in which the waiter can play various games of involvement and placement. Just how much of the interior is revealed through the wide mouth is the backdrop to these games.

Equally sophisticated is the medieval device of the porch, although it possesses quite different characteristics. The outer opening is probably quite large and the porch itself a substantial room. You enter at right angles to the grain of the nave or hall through the second door, which is small, and thus the combination of sudden release of space and change of direction gives maximum cause for awe. Moreover, the smallness of the inner door leaves the power and continuity of the great room intact. It is not so different from the effect of entry into a theatre from the small side doors. In the middle territory lie buildings where the entrance is a strong marker and the internal vestibule a key part of the building, although the two are not visible to each other.

When designing, most of us seem to reach a point where the plan and structure have been established. There may be a fairly advanced idea of the external mannerisms that will develop, but only then do we start to gather in the ingredients for the statement of the mouth. We become conscious of its articulation, or lack of it, nervous (in the case of a streetside building) that the passer-by might miss our building. At this point in history we probably feel some obligation to celebrate and reveal the inside atmosphere. We might regard the doorway as the place in which to play games of scale or hierarchy. To be sure, the act of one or more people coming bodily into our building is of more drama and importance than pushing a window up for a little more air.

Thus, we can note the fundamental issue of value related to architectural event. The other issue most often being played out in the composition of entrances is the pictorial aspect. The flat graphics and the facade mathematics become a balancing act. Classical and other axis-based facades badly need the entrance element. Only in some Art Nouveau houses do we have the quaint experience of another great major orifice having more grandeur – the grand salon window pushing the doorway into a suppressed role. In Modernist architecture of a certain scale there is also a habit of leaving the entrance as a minor element in a pressed condition, possibly even 'grounded' into the solid base below the main architecture which comprises a clear, loose superstructure of glass.

The development of plate glass allied to twentieth-century notions of health and openness contributed to the evolution of the 'inside-outside' concept whereby the skin of the enclosure is developed towards a mechanically supported ambiguity regarding when and where the building ends. The conditions fold into each other and thus the business of entry is consigned to history (though climate and

Savoy Hotel, Ole Bull, Oslo, 1927

Mathildenhöhe, JM Olbrich, Darmstadt, 1907

Old castle, Würzburg

Doctor's villa, Le Corbusier, La Plata, 1949

Street corner, Nara

Mathildenhöhe, JM Olbrich, Darmstadt, 1907

Paula Modersohn-Becker House, Bernhard Hoetger, Bremen, 1926

Paris Metro entrance, Hector Guimard, c1900

Fastloff House, JW Cockrill, Great
Yarmouth, 1912

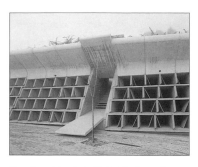

Cemetery at Igualada, Enric Miralles and
Carme Pinos, 1985

Mathildenhöhe, JM Olbrich,
Darmstadt, 1907

Hagbarth Schytte-Berg Pharmacy,
Alesund, Norway, 1906

Staatsgalerie, Stirling and Wilford, Stuttgart,
1983

Masaharu Takasaki Showroom, Tokyo, built
1986, destroyed 1990

Entrance, Peachtree Center, John Portman,
Atlanta, 1985

security tend to disclose the need for some kind of door in the end).

The Australian architect Glen Murcutt responds consciously to the way in which Aborigines wish to enter buildings – glancingly, almost stealthily and at a shallow angle – which opens up the question that in 'educated' civilisations, the business of entering is probably treated in too humdrum a way.

Announcement Within

The entry made, one might hope that the building is conscious of the freshness with which the situation can now be regarded. The outside of the building has sent out various signals. How much will they be able to recognise within? There is the opportunity to refocus and the first encountered inner space has a key role to play. In highly diagrammatic or geometric plans this space might be a pivot; in axial plans the space will be at the centre of a system. However, such plans often lack subtlety.

There can be a number of ways in which the architecture or certain working elements can be proffered to immediately give clues, reassurance and keep the newcomer moving as he comes into the building. The nineteenth-century institutional building is the classic example; an academy or a town hall with a discrete porter's box behind a small window just inside the entrance. There will be one central stair, or two flanking stairs, and the newcomer knows exactly what to do with the minimum number of instructions. With Modernism, the abandonment of the axial plan meant that this obviousness had to be replaced by something better – hence the retention of hierarchy in the size of rooms and the frequent retention of the vestibule. With the advent of freeing the space, fragmenting the parts and bypassing the system of totally contained 'rooms', there remains the necessity to introduce the consequences of entry to the newcomer. Vista becomes more important, as does reference to a contained open space such as a courtyard or a re-entrant open space that can be captured by the wings of the building. Transparent buildings can reveal all to the outside observer who then knows that he must proceed up a ramp, via a bridge, under a box, or whatever. Nonetheless, there is the question of comfortable procedure. You do

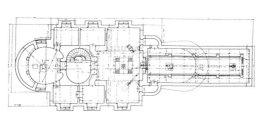

Boston Public Library, Charles Follen McKim, 1887-95

Einstein Tower, Erich Mendelsohn, Potsdam, 1917-21 (plan and photograph)

40

not wish to move onwards and onwards at the same pace. Some remnant of ceremony – or mere 'civility' – remains in the psychology of most people and the building has to respond. A marker might be a change of material, geometry or a conscious 'announcement' within the building. If the doorway itself is an intensification of the manners of the building, then the entrance lobby, vestibule, stairwell or 'hall' (as it would have been in medieval times) also has to make a self-conscious statement.

Perhaps it can establish lines of connection; bands of window, bands of horizontal line, lines of a particular ceiling, treatment or lights, a rising ramp or, of course, the discriminate position of the stair. Commercial rituals suggest that a grand staircase descending from somewhere (often a disappointing space, but effective for the setting of photo-opportunities) becomes essential for a four-star hotel. Even in medium-quality apartment blocks the one place where you can find marble walls is in the entrance vestibule. Organically, the interior of the entrance ensemble can act as a 'catapult' towards the rest of the building. More modestly, it can act as a 'lookout' to the rest of the building.

As an adjunct and as another kind of signal, the vestibule can offer vertical views (that were perhaps not expected from the outside). Circumstantial association of a rising staircase with a series of balconies running around is a common gambit in larger buildings – leading to the common use of the 'atrium' whereby the first encountered space is the dominant space, whereas the rest are small chambers. Even on a domestic scale, the winding-round of the staircase, a roof-light above, or a circuit of doors surrounding you, are useful reference devices.

Aggrandisement and Sequence

How much can the building itself suggest without the need of a plan or a person to advise you? This question need not have been asked in any period up to the early twentieth century where two circumstances combined to reinforce the idea of 'procedure'. The first was the well-mannered response to room hierarchy and geometry; the second, a well-mannered response to social hierarchy. It was not one's place to ferret-around, and it was certainly not one's place to speculate.

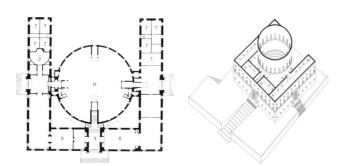

Stockholm Public Library, Gunnar Asplund, 1920-28 (plan and axonometric)

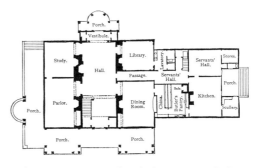

Taylor House, McKim, Meade and White, Newport, Rhode Island, 1885-86

Social and spatial freedom did not inevitably lead to anarchy, however it did lead to confusion from time to time. Today, architects have to be more inventive rather than less. The range and nature as well as the subtlety of signals has to be far more calculated. If a building flows, then the message-giving devices (coloured, sculpted, lit, articulated) have to be designed as such. If a building is highly articulated, then a particular articulation has to be employed to say 'This is where to come', 'This is where to turn', 'This is private', 'This is special'. If a building unfolds – such as the Louisiana Museum near Copenhagen – the unfolding process becomes a theatrical as well a topographical process; spatial, as well as geometrical. In this particular case, the old house at the entrance is retained almost nonchalantly as the most mundane and unceremonious element.

A frequent condition in large buildings is the existence of a major space that is *not* in constant use, coexisting with many other parts that *are* in constant use. This space (perhaps an auditorium, a council chamber, a cafeteria or a viewing terrace) needs to have occasional prominence. The easy but limp option is to give it a separate or parallel entry system to that of the rest of the building. But what if we don't? Elaborate signals have to be sent back to the main entrance area. Almost certainly a third 'foil' condition will be employed such as a courtyard exposing the heroism of the auditorium, or a hint that a certain staircase leads to something pretty important.

In complex buildings, the entrance gambit may be repeated, employing a form of 'A-B-A-B-A-B' sequence whereby 'A' is always the referencing space and 'B', the rest. Urban formations have carried this through, with the existence of repeated rules for the city block and typical articulation of the street corner. The game becomes more interesting if the building climbs, so that the 'A-B' sequence repeats as a system, but the circumstances begin to differ. Without a topographical or induced topographical aid, the incorporation of subtle variations becomes a tricky issue. The unbuilt competition project by Gunnar Asplund and Ture Ryberg for the Royal Chancellery in Stockholm, 1922, executes this procedure brilliantly.

In the planning of circulation, most time is spent keeping the sequence of movement logical and clean. How many architects cut their exploratory sections

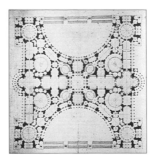

Bâtiment qui contiendrait les Académies, Marie-Joseph Peyre, 1756

Louisiana Museum, Jørgen Bo and Vilhelm Wohlert, Copenhagen, 1958

through the lines of circulation and then through the accompanying set of rooms, thus exploring the possibilities of recognition, vista, sequence, repetition and identity? Once again, the question of 'eye' lines and the procedure through a building as the 'theatre of life' emerges as a topic. Curiously, some of the best periods of architecture for the recognition of the language of space have also been entangled with excessive expressionistic or stylistic complexity. It is as if sensitivity and symbolism are too hot, and that, conversely, the intelligently analytical designer is nervous of formal symbolism. It need not be so. The cinema has been used as a reference and as an inspiration to some late twentieth-century analysts of space. Ways of designing that involve 'vignettes', the drawing of sections in sequence, the tracing of paths and the increased use of computer-generated 'walks' through projected schemes, all point to the evolution of a mode of planning that might escape the tyranny or small-mindedness of the 'net' plan, in itself a respectable but over-modest objective.

Another tactic is to borrow from the principles of cybernetics and programme theory in order to sequence conditions of objects and space in such a way that the user and viewer have a multiplicity of options available within the same assembly of parts. Ademonstratedemonstratedemonstratedemonstrates early as 1964, Cedric Price in London was suggesting with his 'Fun Palace' project that major components such as escalators and ramps could be swung around and that screens could come and go, so that the track of use over space was able to respond to differing conditions or requirements. Since that time, the development of materials and environmental control mechanisms has made even more variations possible. A disarming 'openness' of planning with variable interpretation, such as in an open-plan office or supermarket, is to be seen as a primitive stage in the evolution of the shed, or any other total building.

Axes

We have already come across the dependence of certain types of sequence upon the existence of axis. It seems that centuries of ritual and observance had bound themselves imperceptibly into the instinct of propriety in architecture. There is

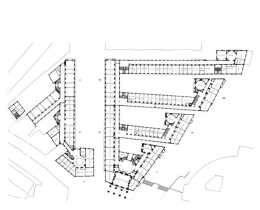

Stockholm Royal Chancellery, Gunnar Asplund and Ture Ryberg, 1922 (competition)

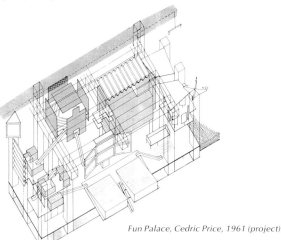

Fun Palace, Cedric Price, 1961 (project)

43

also the train of reasoning that links interpretations of the so-called 'Primitive Hut' from Roman times (Vitruvius) through to Mannerism (Boullée) and Neoclassicism (Chambers). The centralised plan consistently emerges as the development forward from this hut. As Joseph Rykwert writes at the end of his definitive analysis of the Hut myth, *On Adam's House in Paradise*:

> The return to origins always implies a rethinking of what you do customarily, an attempt to renew the validity of your everyday actions, or simply a recall of the natural (or even divine) sanction for your repeating them for a season.

Hierarchy in social organisation, whether through the church, the army or some political development from either, implies a 'head' and its support, or a deity and its worshippers. Allied to this is the 'last bastion' or 'sanctuary' in temples and castles. The roots of the axis are surely there. Add to that the logic of pathways, the manifestation of desire lines – following the star, reaching the mountain or entering the gate. A secondary circumstance places dwellings and resting points either side of the desire line and at once we have an axial system. So far, however, the logic of this does not necessarily suggest equal balance either side of the line. Why should it? For this, we have to return to the issue of imitation of the human body itself, no less; virtual symmetry encompassing the wide differences of individual limbs, orifices, bones or flesh. In its developed form, the axis can be treated as the generator of a whole series of sub-axes. The instinct for order (and if necessary for hierarchy) can be satisfied with elegance.

From the late eighteenth century until the mid-twentieth century, the most developed centre for the art of axial composition was the Ecole des Beaux-Arts in Paris. Strict demands were made with regard to the knowledge of Classical architecture and the playing-out of elaborate exercises of organisation and the celebration of organisation in the form of domes, pavilions, colonnades, halls, vestibules and terraces. The results are magnificent, even if they do appear self-contained and abstractly indulgent by today's scale of values.

In Charles Percier's *Une Edifice à rassembler les Académies* of 1786, total pattern is exploited. The subordinate parts are complete axial buildings in themselves, compounding to surround the grand domed core on three of its sides and then permitting a veritable king of porched spaces to front the fourth side. However, a Beaux-Arts system can equally well explode so that in Julian Guadet's *Un Hospice dans les Alpes* of 1864, there is a proliferation of arms, of both solid building and terracing. Interestingly, the form given to all of this is medieval rather than High Renaissance (perhaps with reference to the mythology of the Alps) suggesting that by this time, the École was concerned with the generation of system rather than style.

Underlying such a tradition, and almost all subsequent essays in the 'axial', is the necessary association of symmetry with power, or order emanating from power. The axes set up by the 'Great' houses of Europe run far beyond the limits of the house and out into the countryside, picking up a reference to a point on the horizon that may be under the ownership or control of the owner of the house. A certain 'arrogance' is implied in the setting up of a line of reference from a district or a town, or a village, or a turn in the road towards a dominant vista that lines with the centre of a building. It is therefore a recognisable sign of the power-instinct of various regimes to insist upon axial palaces or seats of government, and for these to tend to be neoclassical, if only because that architecture is most able to sustain the sense of order.

Approached from the point of view of the purely picturesque, the establishment of a certain number of balanced (and therefore probably axial) elements is a perfect foil to the wayward, the Romantic or the topographically-based 'flow' of a city or closely subdivided countryside. The English or Tuscan landscape relies heavily upon such a proposition. At an urban level, cities such as Bath or Edinburgh play upon the coincidence of picturesque natural landscape overlaid by climbing and turning terraces, focusing from time to time upon 'set piece' buildings with the appropriate spires or pediments. One of the delights of the architectural explorer is the experience of first glimpsing a fragment of a building (perhaps between other buildings, or between trees) and walking progressively towards it, accumulating the sense that any second the axis or the focus will be revealed. This experience can be repeated within a building and the difference between a merely clever piece of classical planning and a spatially or experientially memorable building lies in the art of sequential revelation; the holding back, the hinting, the games of tantalisation and eventual resolution of the composition

Byways and 'Narrative'

As cultural victims of international suburbia, our senses are possibly dulled by the more subtle examples of architectural composition. They can so easily be misinterpreted as merely 'loose', yet they exist as a necessary parallel condition to that of obvious, geometric order. Buildings can unfold without the need for a 'head and shoulders' relationship. Farms, villages, factories and various other agglomerations are familiar to us. The riding of the landscape, the clinging to the edge of the coast or a highway or a river are equally familiar and, on analysis, reveal a key principal of composition; the linear thread is supremely satisfying

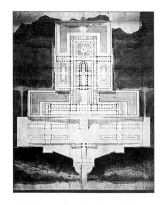

Un Hospice dans les Alpes, Julien Guadet, 1864

Blickling Hall, Robert Lyminge, Norfolk, 1616-1627

Katsura Imperial Palace, Kyoto, from 1590 (interior)

45

and supremely accommodating. The route can wind, change elevation or even hive off at a tangent, yet the system of reference is maintained. In all likelihood, as the means of access, it is the means of survival.

Imperceptibly, this pragmatic circumstance has become immeshed into the aesthetic process. There is no clear dividing line between buildings that string along together and parts of the same building, with an array of internal occurrences that also do so. Paths, corridors, spine walls may assist the process, but are not organically inevitable. The sequential process probably exists within and can be associated with a similar sequence of 'revelation' that was discussed in terms of axiality. Yet it now takes on a greater role. In the unfolding but geometrically random building, the memorable quality of a single chamber or a change of scale must take the place of hierarchy (which was a much easier game to learn). It can be argued that the surprises and subtleties of loose-limbed architecture are richer, more charming or more enigmatic, but they almost certainly put a greater pressure on both the inventiveness and the control of the designer, and are more likely to bewilder him on first approach. In the case of the Louisiana Museum, this has been developed consciously with the parts held contiguously. In the development of Japanese palaces, temples and their gardens, a similar chain of pursuit exists, although without the existence of continuous building. A major part of the sequence occurs in the open air, but the process runs on, springing from built element to built element and often encompassing several shifts of orientation.

A predilection of so-called 'expressionist' composition has been the setting-down of rooms of assorted geometry along a spine that will deflect from time to time. Often there is an accompanying programme that composes these rooms in series and with dramatic deviations, much as in a musical composition in which the linearity of the forward movement is repeated, accentuated or contrasted as it moves onward. If the parts of the building are well understood, if the role that each of them plays is weighed up and given relative value, and if this is accompanied by a clever accentuation of elements, then the expressionist method can be adopted. It can be a subtle as well as a responsive method. It is not generally recognised that the resulting visual mannerisms of the building don't have to be angular of 'funky'. The important factor lies in the detailed analysis and also in the degree of formal discrimination involved. As a result, there are sloppily developed buildings of the genre that encourage its detractors. Many designers are also terrified of being left with pieces of irregular space on their hands.

A further variant of the 'accrued' plan exists when deliberate interference with the basic contiguity is set up. In urbanism, we are familiar with the notion of alleys and byways that occur against the grain of the major streets. If we extrapolate this towards a system of counter-routes entered through a myriad of doors and porches we start to embark upon a fascinating process. Towards the end of the twentieth century there was a revival of interest in the notion of posing a counter axis against a primary axis. The counter axis would be at a deviant angle (maybe 4, 7, 12 degrees of shift). The origins are consciously

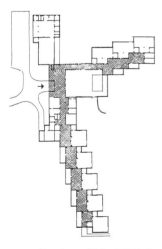

Templewood School, CH Aslin, Welwyn, Hertfordshire, c1950

traceable to Russian Suprematism of the 1920s and if necessary are conveniently adaptable to the insertion of neoclassical elements. It is not too difficult to link this through to the fascination with the idea of 'folding' enjoyed in the l990s and further, to a compositional equivalent of amused near-anarchy predicted in the 1980s. The Wissenschaftcentrum in Berlin by James Stirling and Michael Wilford implodes a series of derived plan-forms together in the manner of a collage. The interactive scatter thus caused needs skilful interpretation into form, for it pressures the parts either to assert themselves (and their origin) as quotation. Alternatively, if all are brought back to an expressionistic commonality, the articulation may be lost.

In the plan forms used by Peter Corrigan (and many of his students in Melbourne) there is a similar conscious anarchy. Beyond, however, there lies a challenge to the stout-hearted: take some of the order and discipline of the Classical tradition, or the strength of axis-making and, with aspects of expressionist responsiveness, ally it in the same building while at the same time employing aspects of relaxed contiguous placement. We might arrive at such a format from the completely different direction – only guessed-at by the author – of processes and myths understood by remote or forgotten civilisations. The Aboriginal sensitivities are now being documented, the mathematics of the prehistoric remnants are subject to theorising, the curious relationships of culture, place, landscape and working parts need constant scrutiny, not in order to mimic them, but in order to sustain our ability to record event via substance.

Whatever mode is adopted – pure or hybrid – there will also be the need for relief and for odd nooks and crannies to be incorporated. The increasing habit of re-adaptation of 'functioning' buildings seems to be coincident with the cultural acceptance of 'fuzzy' logic and institutional and urban 'scatter'. Perhaps at this stage, we need a calm, procedural and measurable sequencing in the approach to buildings, if only to understand how to scramble them.

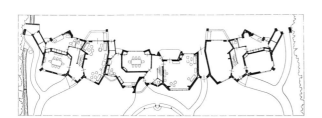

ABOVE: Houses, Peter Lodewijk, Bergen, The Netherlands, 1915-16;
RIGHT: Sapporo Beer Guest House, Toyo Ito, Eniwa, Hokkaido, 1989

CIRCULATION AND PLANNING

Association

The relationship between 'function' and 'common sense' was touched on in Chapter Three and we have already noted the constant departures that are made from the purely logical path of cause and effect, primarily because architecture is riddled with symbolism, prejudice and curious cultural habits. Any group of people wanting a building will probably have existing examples in their minds. Few will be able to handle a totally fresh and original concept without coaxing and an extensive and continual explanation of every move by the architects. Even when a new use-type is required, they will try desperately to associate it with something that already happens. The history of design is full of this syndrome; early motor cars, for example, initially retained many aspects of the horse-drawn carriage and were only able to discard them one-by-one as recognition of the car as a typology took hold.

The architectural equivalents can be even more amusing, partly because all come within the umbrella term 'building' and partly because there seems to be a need for constant reassurance, and a constant reminder of symbols of value. Alongside runs the notion that certain activities should be respected, others concealed from view, yet others announced. The 'Royal Box' or 'Directors Suite' the formal 'Ante Room' at one end of the scale and the alcove in the living room for the display of trophies at the other, may be marginal elements and yet difficult to eliminate from people's minds. Yet only lately has the exposed kitchen or the flimsy changing room become socially (and therefore architecturally) acceptable.

The design process usually starts with a functional grouping of the parts. If left to the architect this will be left unloaded, but if provided by the client or the brief writers for a competition it will begin to have particular loadings. The trick, in fact, is to investigate this loading as much as possible. It may well be that the members of a company board, a committee or a family have not resolved all their political intrigues and that the written instructions are concealing further struggles. All too often the architect becomes the unwitting pawn in a game in which he certainly cannot win. In specialised territories – the design of hospitals, production systems, warehousing, academic buildings, airports, places of

entertainment – there are constantly shifting theories, depending upon the particular expert consulted and their relationship to the organisation. From air movement patterns related in therapy, at one level, to granny's enjoyment of a sunset view at another, a mixture of the strategic and the personal will establish the true brief of the project.

The most sophisticated of clients will even know how to tie up a brief so that a certain type of architecture can be assured. The scanning of a competition brief can therefore be a very intriguing piece of 'detective' work for the architect, who has to sniff out the odd give-away element in a list of straightforward rooms or requirements. 'Approach', 'terrace', 'main level', 'for the general public', 'occasional use' and other such specifications should be pursued immediately and cross-referenced to anything else that starts loading up the evidence of a value system on the part of the client. The person entrusted with the writing of the brief is in a position of great power; the brief itself should be aggressive and coercive in its composition. Even when it is left to the designer, a creative moment exists. Hence it can be valuable to write a number of alternative briefs with differing nuances, lists and challenges which should be argued through intellectually like a chess problem. Alternatives should only be exposed to the client if the architect has full faith in his relationship with the client.

The extent to which there can be a separate strategy for each segment of the building is partly a question of philosophy and partly a question of self-control. Historical precedent suggests that the hierarchies of 'great' buildings were of significant value in the determination of a plan. After all, they reflected the hierarchies of society that were represented within; servants in meagre spaces, ceremony in exaggerated spaces and a 'generosity' of space reflecting the cheapness of labour and thus the multiplication of minor functions that would today be dealt with by domestic or industrial appliances. Certain remnants of the precedent survive, especially the ceremonial carry-over in the ground floor space of city buildings. What else, if not a ceremonial room, is the 'lobby' to a corporate headquarters? What else, if not dismissive, are the facilities for car parking, staff rest rooms, laundry rooms, janitors' rooms or mail rooms in the same building?

Decorative Arts Museum, Richard Meier, Frankfurt, 1984

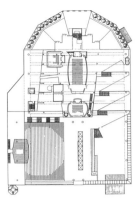

Palazzo del Cinema, Fumihiku Maki, Venice, 1990

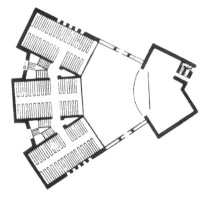

Rusakov Club, Konstantin Melnikov, Moscow 1927

Friedrichstrasse Offices, Mies van der Rohe, Berlin, 1919 version, (unrealised project)

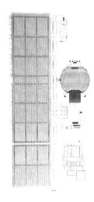

Congress Hall, Fumihiko Maki, Tokyo, 1990

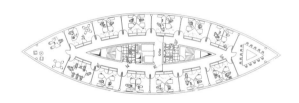

Micro Electronics Park, Norman Foster, Neudorf, Duisberg, 1992

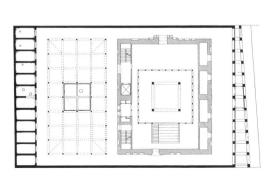

Deutsches Architektur Museum, Oswald Mathias Ungers, Frankfurt, 1965

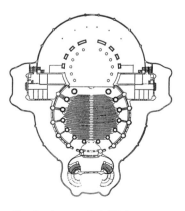

First Goetheanum, Rudolf Steiner, Dornach, 1913-20

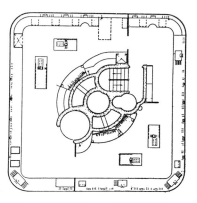

Johnson Wax Headquarters, Frank Lloyd Wright, Racine, Wisconsin, 1936-49

Shonandai Cultural Centre, Itsuko Hasegawa, 1991

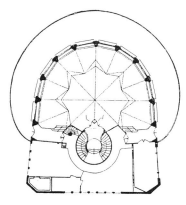

Revolving House, Max Taut, 1920 (project)

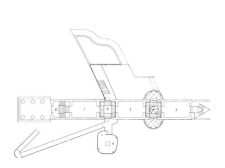

Graphic Art Museum, Arata Isozaki, Okanoyama, 1982

Chapel at Nôtre Dame du Haut, Le Corbusier, Ronchamp, 1950-54

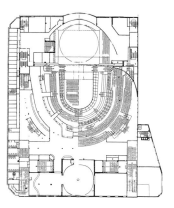

Grosse Schauspielhaus, Hans Poelzig, Berlin, 1918-19

Philharmonie Concert Hall, Hans Scharoun, Berlin, 1956-63

Functional separation, group identification, hierarchical territoriality all relate to each other. At one point, it is worth making a parallel exercise to that of writing and combating alternative briefs; in other words, to 'scramble' the room groupings and 'association' territories simply to see what happens if the boardroom is visible from the entrance, or if the janitor's room is given some pride of place, or some normally hidden functions are celebrated as prominent components of the building. Another tactic is to build in a large amount of 'slack' into the planning. This is not necessarily encouraged by the client's accountants, but again, it is certainly possible in the creative stage of design. One can thus experiment with degrees of space exchange and the possible evolution of hybrids between function-type. In the comparative plans on pages 50-51, there is a separation into 'tight' and 'loose' plans and various categories of association.

Most of the processes described so far can be applied to the whole building. A traditional Oxford or Cambridge college will work in terms of the student rooms and the beadle's point of control. The hall and chapel will remain distinct. Twentieth-century additions will scrupulously adhere to this system of discrimination, whatever the mannerisms of the architecture; the office tower will need the lobby to remain larger volumetrically than anything else in the structure, once again, regardless of the mannerisms of the architecture. One special exception to all this does exist: the ancillary. Such an element can be designed together with the main block and it can be critical in that it is not only separate but of a distinctly different scale (though not style), such as the 'lodge' of a great house or college, or the auditorium of an institution that otherwise demands 'repeats' of rooms and windows, or a small building permitted to exist within the courtyard of the completed block.

Circulation

In the discussion so far, we have encountered movement and the identification of movement where it has been the product of certain motives – of aggrandisement, identification, procession or action that is culturally necessary. At base however, it should be the product of obvious processes demanded by an interpretation of the building brief. Getting around should be a joy. Arriving should be painless and the point of arrival identifiable, if not too predictable in terms of atmosphere. Having determined the grouping of rooms, their relationship is expected to be consistent. It is certainly odd if the same type of rooms in the same building opens off spaces in unexpected ways. Equally, it is very difficult for the newcomer if the progression of rooms is awkward or inconsequential. Such an experience can be found in places where, for instance, a series of separate houses have been converted into a hotel or into a school. Suddenly, the circulation space that in the past had some 'local' significance (in relation to the habits of a small family) becomes incidental in the sequence of activities of large numbers of people. The small rooms themselves work well but the lead-up is lost. In this commonplace example we see that the 'pulse' of a building is the concern. Circulation is not just a linear issue, but concerns marking, pausing and celebrating as much as any other 'conditioner'. Circulation is about getting there, but buildings can almost be divided into two categories: first, those in which the procedure from the entrance to the room in which you will spend most time is a crashing bore, a forgettable experience, etc; secondly, those in which the business of working your way towards your destination is a memorable and episodic experience. The stay in the room is predictable, so the wish to escape from it and return to the rest of the building – in order to ferret around and discover more – might take over. Undoubtedly there are buildings in which the balance is held, yet the calculation of impact is extremely hard to control. A standard functioning type – such as bedroom, laboratory, kitchen or recreation room – has to be respected. The business of moving upwards by one storey, changing direction around a courtyard, pausing to deal with a bifurcation of routes (incorporating the garden wing or the terrace wing, or more mundanely, the routes towards the goods entrance or towards the cloakrooms) can rarely be left at the level of the built diagram. The possible glimpse of the courtyard, the three-dimensional potential of the climb upwards, the difference of light coming in from the garden as opposed to that of the terrace, the comings and goings of the goods coming through the goods entrance and the inherent shyness associated with going off to the toilet all have spatial and dimensional potential for the designer.

Thus, the interchange of value or architectural 'pace' between the circulatory parts and those elements that are on the receiving end of that circulation is a problem that demands a thoughtful overview on the part of the designer. It is a question of sequence, position and articulation all at once, but it involves declamation. As if one might say 'We are going to move towards the gymnasium', 'Now we are near the gymnasium', 'Look! There's a view of the lake', and finally 'This is the gymnasium'. It is easy to say that the lead-up might overwhelm the eventual goal, but a series of dull doors along a corridor of which the last is marked 'gymnasium' is hardly the answer.

Once an attitude towards such sequencing is arrived at and the grouping of rooms determined, their relationship should be consistent. It is intriguing if some rooms open off tiny corridors, some off long corridors and some off random

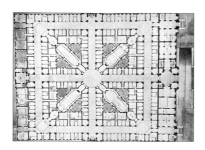

Covered fair, Antoine-François Peyre, 1762

Sumida Culture Factory, Itsuko Hasegawa, Tokyo, 1990-92

lobbies, yet all in the same part of the building. It would be the result of carelessness (or in the case of one building in ten thousand, a piece of creative virtuosity) from which we can draw no conclusions. There could be, however, a section of the building in which the special nature of the oddly-shaped lobby and a series of identifiable room-to-corridor relationships suggests a very particular set of activities. On occasion, the sheer unexpectedness of a circulatory item can set the scene for a heightened response to the mere business of getting-around. In a building that is already rich with vitality, the audience at the Berlin Philharmonic is seduced upwards by a series of oddly angled staircases and is thus prepared for the progressive 'scatter' as it moves upwards into the auditorium. The geometry used is consistent, but the gambits evolve one by one as you progress. In such a building, circulation can be sensed as a flowing and organic activity; essentially dynamic rather than merely linear. Circulation is often dealt with as a hierarchical issue. The human frame remains a constant measurable item. People can comfortably climb a 40 degree staircase, but are also conveniently agile for turning 45, 90 or even 135 degrees away from their previous route. They could if they wanted, squeeze through a 15 centimetre gap, but are more accustomed to one of 80 centimetres. These are the bald facts. The generous dimensions of the grand vestibule contrasted with the narrow passages backstage in a theatre tell of society rather than measure. Some common examples may give clues to the issue.

The Office Building

Primary circulation will be designed from the lift-stack outwards. Since the building is not often designed specifically for a particular office occupant, the most mundane of 'compartmented', 'open plan' versions will have been assumed. Fire protection will encourage the designer to separate the space immediately facing the lifts from the main floor areas. From this point onwards, we are faced with a building that lacks continuity, where the experience of the whole can rarely benefit from the accumulation of local experiences. The predictability of the entry sequence also helps to deaden the impact. Once within the compartment however, interesting things may begin to happen. Recent developments suggest that there are many

Philharmonie Concert Hall, Hans Scharoun, Berlin, 1956-63 (entrance area)

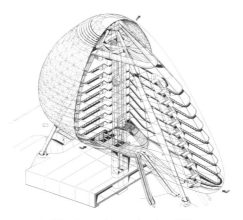

Green Building, Future Systems, London, 1991

DE Shaw Company Office, Stephen Holl, New York, 1991-92

hybrids available between the row of 3.5 metre hutches or the single space interrupted by low screens and rubber plants. The sociology of the office develops – the boss/secretary breakdown already has a dated, early twentieth-century sound to it – as too does the need for ambiguously defined 'semi-circulatory' spaces. To share spaces where an intense activity (a discussion involving money and resources for example) might take place at one time and a 'loose' activity (the dumping of shopping bags) take place at another would have been unthinkable in the past, but are now potentially rich, not only as signals of emancipation, but as instigators of new attitudes towards building use. Because the independent 'office' or enterprise of that type exists with the evolving world (it is not insulated in the same way as a bureaucracy or an institution such as a police force or a college), it can flex and flow. In addition, the partitions can be pulled out overnight, the outfit may go bust or the building shell be relet.

We can draw creatively from this model. For example, a floor-plate delineated with series of 'patches' of space with a range of overlaid uses enables circulation to give the inmates perhaps three or four different ways to move around, exerting nuance and preference rather than the inevitable journey up the corridor to Room 217. The three-dimensional extension of such a philosophy is harder to achieve, but may also develop.

The Market Hall

Basically a shelter for an activity, this typology can be allied to that of exhibition halls, certain types of museum and even bus garages. The objective is to stack together a series of equal 'stalls', make them accessible, feed them efficiently and then maybe celebrate the total volume as an identifiable icon in the city. The main entry should enable the buyer to confront as many routes as possible at the first move, and he should be able to depart quickly once he has finished his business. In a parallel sequence (though perhaps at a different time of day) the supplier or the trader needs to bring in goods as effortlessly as possible. A rectilinear grid, like a city grid, is the normal answer. Strangely, however, it is very rare for the hall to do more. If only clues could be taken; for example, the plan of bourgeois Barcelona, where the existence of the diagonal and the occasional geometrical interference makes the gridded system all the more magical. Greater use of the ramp or of descending into the space could serve both to spatialise and identify the parts. In exhibition halls, the need for this is even greater than in market buildings. In the development of factories and television studios, recourse to the ceiling as a location for gantries and lighting or platform grids has led to the idea of the working space as a 'sandwich' existence between two layers of access and service. From this we can be conveniently reminded that circulation is not necessarily a question of facility fed from a single layer. Most likely, people will have to occupy the main plane whilst goods, equipment, removable built parts, lighting and energy will arrive via another plane. Traditionally, few architects have designed plans with the knowledge of the ceiling grid sitting in their minds, but this can change in time and is certainly worth the mental agility involved.

The School

As the link between learning and separation from the bustle of the city developed over the twentieth century, the tendency to place schools in open space and away from the intense centres of population has coerced the morphology of the school building itself to being a collection of attenuated elements, at least four of which comprise classrooms (often in significant groupings), the gymnasium, laboratories and the administration facilities. These parts are posed deliberately towards the surrounding open spaces as much as they are posed towards each other, and probably more so. The business of proceeding from one to the other is therefore a lineal, strung-out business. Yet, it is not just the occasional controlled and judicious person that is strolling along between the rooms. It is a sudden, swinging surge of twenty or thirty sets of arms and legs! In a school building the idea of circulation as 'slack' becomes significant. The idea of the concentrated patch of space is essential – smells, sounds, designated equipment, controllable space – are all the ingredients of the 'room'. The total building can afford to wear its heart on its sleeve and the total formality resembles a piece of city rather than a balanced, tight building. In the case of the school for Pomona, California, Morphosis create a series of hybrid typologies that fold together between the traditions of 'yard', 'room', 'terrace', 'enclave' and 'pad'; and in so doing they need to be related by (and to receive) a stronger diagrammatic network.

The late twentieth-century school complex (or campus complex) along with certain categories of industrial plant that contain disparate elements, all set forth one of the fundamental theorems of framework circulation. The more systematic the net of routes, the more idiosyncratic the individual pieces may be. Conversely, the less comprehensible the linking system, the greater the need for the rooms to be clear and simple, and probably similar to each other. Ignorance of this is not only some form of conceptual anarchy, but simply a chaotic building. In extremely developed cases, there can be a magical link between the idea of views through the building and routes through the building, certainly not occurring on the same lines but in a contrapuntal relationship with each other. So, we raise the issue (from another direction) that circulation *per se* is a useful starting point for the strategisation of a building, but not at all self-sufficient as the determining element of 'place' or 'weight' or 'presence'.

The Hotel

The individual hotel room is relatively small and definable and its organisation and relationship to the outside world well known. Thus, surely the organisation of the resulting building is predictable? Once again, however, circulation is affected by the gestural issues at work in a building that must represent a series of different worlds to different people – for example, those who want a simple night's rest as distinct from those who are celebrating the break from their normal routine in the family home. The public spaces also reflect a series of overlaid worlds; the servicing of the guests and the provision of facilities offered to an often bland and restricted community immediately surrounding the hotel, in addition to the chance to add a touch of glamour, to escape or to offer a higher level of servicing. Then there is the hotel as a temporary adjunct to the business of selling or informing, which is similar in its activity to showroom or college when within the territory of giving conferences. Before the list of overlays is complete, we must add the annual Ball and the whist drive, as well as the cat show! Directing a drunken guest and bringing through a prize cat must be assessed in terms of entrances, exits, corridor widths and lengths. So too must the *tête-à-tête* dinner and the quick snack provided for by the same refrigerated room, and remember the old 'concierge' point of the small hotel – which controls access to the lifts and stairs – and the fast exit of the slippery guest. But systems of circulation start to stretch once the swimming pool and its terraces take over from the traditional courtyard, or while the flow of conference delegates may well be eight times the maximum possible impact of hotel guests at breakfast time.

What we are looking at, therefore, are two coincidental factors. First, the overlay of several sets of desire lines on the part of the users: the casual guest becomes more insistent at breakfast time; the passer-through becomes both more sloppy and more inquisitive at the end of the formal conference period and progressively so as the input of drinks begins to take effect. The second fact is that these several sets of desire lines may have to be adaptable to additional or alternative entrance conditions, sudden reversals of flow as well as the seasonal response to hot weather or late-night activities.

The designer of the hotel has tremendous opportunities for invention and dexterity in this world. It is surprising that so many late twentieth-century hotels are formulaic and seem to give up after the provision of the atrium space in plan and section. Interestingly though, from the small-scale end there is a major challenge. The idea of the hotel as functioning office is upon us. The demands of the office-as-suite will develop the possibility of the hotel-as-dwelling which has already been available to a few since the nineteenth century. Combine the potential of these two, add to it the endless extension of events from conferences through demonstration, seminar, exhibition, simulation to virtual reality experience, and at once we have the model of an alternative city suggested by contemporary experience. Equally, it may be that our habits of movement, demarcations of time and assumptions of role begin to be broken down in the hotel. The issue of circulation becomes a marker, a cipher for the immediate architectural context of the future.

The Hospital

Since it can literally be a matter of life and death, the circulation system of a hospital would seem to be the model for logical and dispassionate issues of organisation, yet it is a known fact that certain patients develop positive and negative responses to the sequence of events in traumatic situations. More commonly, they seem to recover more happily in certain locations than in others. Hence we face the issue of 'cold' circulation and 'loaded' circulation; the 'cold' logic of a plan and the overlaying of another pattern of preference, locational paranoia, withdrawal in addition to fairly obvious issues of the view of the river or green fields, trees and the like. The designer can actually perform a series of overlays of predictable psychological responses to various otherwise equivalent locations. 'Where is the best spot?' is a more serious extension of the question 'Can I have the best table?' at a restaurant.

Paths

The discussion of paths seems to crop up regardless of starting point, yet the plotting of paths needs to be constantly redefined. At the core of the issue of circulation, they offer us a cerebral clue to the meaning and purpose of our designs, analytical, measurable and able to be extracted and distilled from the rest of the design process; intention without loading, energy without circumstance. But this is not necessarily so. It is possible to carry out the creative equivalent of the mathematical or scientific proposition through the statement of an equation. In the architectural version, the 'niceness' of a plan will not suffice; it must be loaded with a rich variety of predictions and visualisations. This is now significantly possible by making computer predictions. Even so, the circulatory sequence is most likely to be the common reference as well as a prime generator. Passing through a building is not an evenly-loaded experience. Equally, the path is not a 'flat' condition. In most buildings we climb and descend, meander and dally. Too few architects design their path systems in three dimensions; having a bland tendency to repeat a 'neat' layout of one floor onto the next despite differences of use and spatial experience. If nothing else, recent technological and material developments suggest that the local distribution of walls and partitions or servicing systems can be variously tapped or rejigged from floor to floor. The envelope that can be reinterpreted is not merely a philosophic goal, it is a practicality that challenges the reiteration of the 'dumb' plan or the 'standard' room. Have we grown used to the twentieth century in our attitude towards planning? Only in airports does there seem to be any response to the needs of both the hustler and the crawler. Perhaps it is here that they have both made their presence known, the hustler in particular. The idea of the fast track and the coincidence of the

Palm Court – Britannia Hotel, Trondheim, c1930

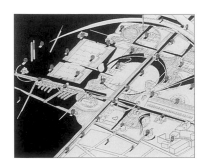

Parc de la Villette, Bernard Tschumi, 1986

Conservatoire de Musique, Christian de Portzamparc, Paris, 1984

travelator alongside the normal path should act as a clue. Analogies can be made with 'bright' and 'gloomy' zones, or 'hard' and 'soft' aesthetics (or upholstery). Intensity and the release of intensity could, if we so wished, be the forerunner of subtle planning. Let us think for a moment of a territory in a building that is moved through on two axes, one 'fast' and the other 'slow'. Let us assume that one of these paths is strong on identification and iconography, perhaps focusing on a heroic element. Let us also assume that the 'slow' condition is encased in a different form of architecture from the 'fast'; it is full of nooks and crannies, it is pulled up onto a subsidiary level and it is lit less strongly. Let us add to this the possibility that the two conditions focus organisationally on different aspects of the building. In this hypothetical example, the path is the key to a whole series of interpreted consequences, the only addition to its traditional creative role concerning the range of consequences.

In so many ways, the paths that run through a building focus down from our experience of the big city and our wish to both enjoy it and pervert it. As we become more iconoclastic as a civilisation we crave a system that will inhibit or control us less. Out of that could come (at least conceptually) an individually-interpreted city. So why not an individually-interpreted building? Sure, we have such a thing in the rediscovered and reused historical structure, but the radicalism of the present proposal lies in our intentions. Could there be an architecture with endless paths of activity?

Systems

In comparing the 'classic' examples of eighteenth, nineteenth, early and late twentieth-century planning, I am basing the analysis on cultural typicality. In the previous spread of plans, I deliberately chose the mavericks, although this is a difficult territory in which to be really helpful. The connoisseur is attracted almost automatically to those plans in which the apparent orthodoxy of a period is subverted (cleverly, of course) by a few deft moves that offer significance to a moment in the passage through the building. My own preference is for visual or theatrical bonuses rather than elegant tricks of the plan's geometry for their own sake. The fineness of a system however, may well be related to the degree of range of spaces, rooms and manoeuvres made possible by a classical 'ordering' of that system, in the same frame of satisfaction as the exploration of the potentiality of the key of D minor by a composer.

In the earlier systems of organisation there is inevitably a tight relationship between the creation of passages and the delineation of structure. There is a tendency to subscribe the more immediate demarcation of rooms to the creation of major blocks that could be completed and roofed without deformation. Rectilinearity is thus both proper in the sense of manners as well as circumspect in the sense of construction. If the circle is added to the vocabulary, it is done at a sufficient scale to absorb the problems of construction in solid materials. The circular event in the plan is almost always celebrated by a major route which enjoys the act of perambulation that is involved with changing views. By the

Victorian period, the reliance upon fundamental forms and dominant geometries of organisation was so clearly under threat that we can 'read' the episodic nature amongst the 'chatter' suggested by many plans, even though the preoccupation with axes has hardly diminished. Greater virtuosity of engineering and the use of iron and steel are factors, so the inevitability of the paths and corridors as dictates of the organisation begin to break down as well. The notion of continually enclosed space becomes a reality and, with it, the likely realisation that the structural interval can be a mere interference and not a cage. The emancipation of reinforced concrete seemed, in many cases, to mark a return to the 'chamber' and the celebration of encompassing geometries. Except in certain expressionist buildings, the orthodoxy of geometries is rather surprising; for many, the use of concrete perhaps meant no more than an exploitable reincarnation (with less bother) of masonry. The celebration of the ramp has to be seen as a significant explosion of the inherited structures of organisation and the point at which architectural circulation rediscovered creativity, as understood by the Egyptians and Assyrians. Melnikov's audacious project for a garage of one thousand cars in Paris is a series of stacked diagonals sweeping upwards over the Seine; an example of continuous 'rampery' that is effectively the whole building. Less than five years later (1928-30) the ramps of Le Corbusier's Villa Savoye were taking on the key role of both organisation and iconography, and Le Corbusier was consciously returning to the ramped ziggurat of Mesopotamia in his 1929 project for a world museum. By the mid-1930s, the idea of the diagonal as a generator of both plan and section was well within the language of progressive architects, whether in the loaded sense of Melnikov's Narkomtiazprom building of 1934 or the more relaxed emergence of them in several of Hans Poelzig's projects. The ramp is the start of the unstoppable progress of the system to free itself from being a two-dimensional issue – along with the lift and, more appropriately, the escalator. Thus, the possibility of continuous exploration of the building along-and-upwards, as opposed to by 'layers', becomes achievable and must merely wait for enough brave souls to get their analytical minds around it. The notion of the folding surface – or even something as disciplined as the escalator ribbon that renders

House, Itsuko Hasegawa, Nerima,1985-86

Sainsbury Centre, Norman Foster, University of East Anglia, Norwich, 1978

Villa Savoye, Le Corbusier, Poissy, 1928-31

the system of Piano and Rogers' Centre Pompidou three-dimensional – is made possible, although analysis of architecture can never be quite so simplistic.

Human patterns of movement, based on common sense and laziness, demand that a building be accessible and recognisable, at least on the second or third try. A lift, though rarely thought of as a delight, will be readily used when it is convenient. Such an assumption results in replicated planning. A ramp often thought of as a delight has the advantage of encouraging the 'reading' of large swathes of the building, but is often disliked by the 'money men' because it takes up more space and perhaps because it reveals and thus calls attention to uncared-for pockets.

In the twentieth century the ramp has also accelerated its impact by virtue of the number of buildings that contain parking in the basement and by the gradual insistence that public buildings be accessible to wheelchair users. The possibilities for 'warping' the surfaces of the building and for 'releasing' the space have only been realised by a few. If this is considered to be an issue of plasticity as well as linearity, it can be considered a major breakthrough in the way in which space, form, movement and material technique are involved together. It is possible to take the 'road' into a building, as well as to take paths onto (and into) a building, to set a building along a climbing path and to weave paths and roads around a building. Thus, the old demarcations between 'street' and 'site' have fallen away.

Minimum Movement and the Unknown Neighbour

So far, I have accepted the traditions of reading, acting and marking a building that served adequately – that is until electronics and electrics really took hold. In the 1920s, only a few responded to the impact of electricity and its creative possibilities in housing. In Frankfurt, the public housing that came under the direction of Ernst May contained specially-developed kitchens and bathrooms that fully integrated the appliances and techniques of the day. Architects of the fifties such as Charles and Ray Eames, Buckminster Fuller and Alison and Peter Smithson made inspired responses to 'the appliance'. Subsequently, the incorporation of packaged elements and domestic circulation that takes advantage

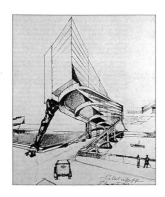

Parking garage over the Seine, Konstantin Melnikov, Paris, 1925 (project)

Highway Housing, George Heinrichs, Berlin, 1970-72

of forced air supply has become commonplace with the result that the interior of an apartment is most likely to contain bathrooms and kitchens that are far from windows. Larger buildings contain service spaces that can be stacked into the middle of the building and are similarly supported by forced air and artificial light. The effects of this upon circulation and space are progressive and we begin to reach an attitude that accepts 'primary' and 'secondary' environments. This is not for the first time. Did not the Victorian villas contain two sets of circulation and standards of space, one for the gentry and the other for the servants? Our contemporary demarcation is between circulation and space for the 'support' activities of storing, servicing, supplying and preparing (so that in the case of a kitchen or laundry people are still back/down there) and the 'front' activities of working, learning, selling are situated with the appropriate atmosphere. A glance at the plans of many quite enlightened projects will reveal the acceptable 'double-think'. At this point we establish a link between circulation, space and atmosphere, as well as with mechanical facility.

In the modern world, much time is spent in cars. They are able to contain extremely elaborate stereo sound, sensitive air conditioning, air-responsive upholstery and their circulation pattern is infinite. The structure of cities should declare the position of flight-paths, radar traps, cable television paths and the like as they do the position of streets and churches. Our own rooms begin to absorb Internet cables and outlets. Drink machines can handle six to ten beverage flavours in both 'hot' and 'cold' modes. Watch the patterns that begin to emerge from all of this. The 'study' of Edwardian times is now the personal computer. The 'listening space' for Beethoven quartets may be the front seat of the car, the key link of the house may not be the front door but the removable services panel. We have long ago recognised the replacement of the hearth by the television set, but now this in itself has become a multiplied element found all over the house. The kitchen may be only one point of reference for the hungry or thirsty. In office buildings this dispersal and universality of location runs in parallel. The plotting of the path of circulation now has more to do with desire or coercion than optimisation; no longer must we use a particular room in a building in a

Imagination Building, Ron Herron, London, 1987-89

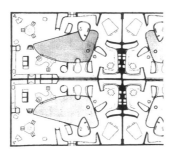

House of the Future, Alison and Peter Smithson, 1956

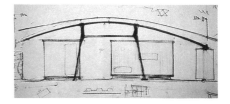

Tropical House, Jean Prouvé, 1949

particularly sequenced or even specific way. The disturbing corollary to this is that the occupant no longer needs to move about from place to place. A counteraction might, therefore, be a redefinition of circulation much more akin to the idea of a 'theme' or 'programme' that we have in a theatre or set-up for a day's television output. A building might contain 'paths' or sequences of incident – doors, lights, special conditions of available space – which are also capable of being changed, hidden, revealed or disposed of cybernetically.

A product of the same cultural shift is the deliberately 'faceless' agency building, such as that which lies alongside Frankfurt Airport, where you can rent a compartment and as much servicing as you wish and thereby establish a 'presence' in the centre of Europe for your firm. The presence might almost be electronic in terms of involvement. Nonetheless, from time-to-time, there is the intrinsic need for the chance of human presence. In conjunction with the nearby hotel and, of course, well-appointed airports with restaurants, food stores and night-clubs, it sets a marker for a new typology – the inter-networked 'available presence' building. Circulation can be optional, variable, celebratory or even virtual. Why not just make yourself comfortable in the chair? The interfaces will emerge! Far from recoiling from the prospect, my only concern is that some of the most creative architectural minds are not yet involved in such projects.

There is real potential in dealing with the chameleon-surfaced, fully robotised, 'non-organisational' organisation. Consider for example, the idea of an architecture set up like a huge beehive with an intelligence like a giant set of flight-paths and circulation patterns that becomes optional or available in different guises according to taste. The interface with the car is part of all this; the car available just outside the door, as an adjunct to the rest of the facility. Thus, in one interrelated sweep, we bypass the concepts of 'street', 'institution', 'workplace', 'inside', 'outside', 'car park', etc. Circulation, as such, is replaced by programme.

Glass Bridge, Peter Rice and Ian Ritchie, Paris, 1985

'Cushicle', Michael Webb, 1965 (project)

'Robohouse', Ron Herron, 1985 (project)

JOINING

Articulation or Solidity?

The carcass of a structure is the dominant condition from which everything else stems. At the centre of the shell lies the typical condition – large or small rooms, progressions of event or reiteration of a standard condition – that result in the same basic output. An entrance condition will develop towards a system of circulation. So far these have been discussed as complete sets. In fact, there are many buildings that do not have such completeness (even those that are conceived as a whole) for the inevitable question of 'elements' comes into play.

We recognise the identification of elements such as 'coffee shop', 'gymnasium', 'boiler room', 'laboratory block' or 'caretaker's house' since they are function-based and have immediate implications of scale and 'publicness'. But let us suppose that the laboratory block has demands that are similar to the rest of a research institution building with the same demands for servicing, access, light and the rest. Do we search hard for something special about laboratory activity? Are we, for example, searching for three large rooms that can be three large lumps greeting the skyline? Before answering the question I will set up a parallel question. Let us suppose that this research institution runs alongside a busy highway and backs onto a garden. Clearly, the two faces can be dealt with differently – small windows in a solid wall on the road side and a more open relationship with the garden. In no time at all, the designer is coercing the corridor that links the laboratories towards the road side and looking for other excuses to 'load' the circulation, not to the middle, but to one side. Combining the two intentions, we begin to get an articulate and lopsided building. The designer remembers that each laboratory needs a supervisor's private office, and easily argues that this (small) room does not need to have the same kind of atmosphere or ceiling height as the labs themselves. The rest is easy. There is an A-B-A-B-A-B syncopation of the rooms and in the other direction there is B, which is large and airy, alongside the corridor and C, which has a dense wall alongside the road. Two more consequences are that the views from the corridor may be through the laboratories, suggesting an internal glass wall and some nifty articulation of the small offices in relation to the corridor.

Another architect, however, would find this whole effort tiresome; aesthetically and intellectually unnecessary. Whilst still noting the highway and the garden, this person will hold the parts in control, will have determined that a central corridor is the system for the whole building and will organise the three laboratories and the three offices in another way. Perhaps the offices will run together to act as a fourth equal part with the other three rooms. Most probably the idea of an articulated skyline will also seem unnecessary to this designer. Keeping with the story, we can now speculate upon the different ways in which this laboratory block might be joined, horizontally to other parts of the institution. The first designer may well enjoy the act of separating and therefore getting more skyline changes. The second designer may wish for a solid, consistent statement to be made by the block and wish it to be articulated clearly from anything on the site. A few designers will prefer some apparently 'seamless' weave of the laboratories into the rest. In this anecdote, I have suggested that articulation is a question of expression as much as anything else. The business of joining stems differs from the business of stating the components themselves and has a certain 'rhythmical' character, which lets the junctions act in the same way as punctuation in a piece of writing. The trained architect follows the conventions of order and distinction in a way that is remarkably similar to the traditions of the farmer or the soldier. There is the grouping together of items of similar size and quality. There is the ranging of forces together or in patterns of interdependent value. Simply extrapolate the pros and cons of grazing sheep in similar fields to cows, or the flanking of infantry by artillery or vice-versa and you have the circumstantial planning of a building. With fabric however, you have issues of continuity and stability, not to speak of style involving itself with the apparent logic of 'sets'. The appeal of 'fuzzy logic' theory to architects lies in its essentially anarchic stance in regard to 'set' procedures. When predictable organics seem to ask for a completed set of parts and junctions, the designer often feels trapped.

Association and 'Signals'

If certain assumptions are made for the way in which well-known user-types each have their organic characteristics we should always be on the look out for exceptions. Those exceptions have an interesting habit of being the significant architecture of their period. But to establish the points of departure, it can first be assumed that domestic architecture is made up of small rooms. The need for privacy and cosiness come together, as well as a certain degree of inherent traditionalism with regard to the function of bedrooms, kitchens and the rest. Next is the predictable hierarchy displayed by institutional buildings; heroic entrances, heroic council chambers, repeatable small offices. On another tack, the lineality of a manufacturing process usually has to be respected by the sequence of parts and their tight, kebab-like adherence to the processional route. In churches, theatres or certain types of conference centre, ritual is the dictating force of the plan. The key ritualistic chamber is of a major scale and, of course, in a precisely understood moment in the sequence of use.

We have already seen that articulation or interruption does not always have to occur for functional reasons, but certain typologies are demanding. An architect offering a single barn-like space for a family would need to know that family pretty well to propose such a thing. Similarly, to recommend the deviation of an established manufacturing sequence suggests that the architect turns manufacturer rather than acts as interpreter of a given programme. Yet we can observe some marvellous interpretations of the question 'How can I recognise my apartment from the rest in the block?'. History also contains instances of the architect who, in the course of intelligently analysing the brief of an industrial operation, returns with a reappraisal of the bad habits that have been acquired, assumed or inherited and are simply waiting to be edited out. In both cases, the resultant building has more to do with figure responding to statement than to stylisation.

It is possible to reinterpret an institution such as a town hall or a school as an assembly of interdependent activities as most of them work around known and consistent groups of people. Universality can be claimed and with the scattering of services and equipment, almost universal provision can be brought to any part of the building's surface. Theoretically, there is no need for interruption, articulation or joining. The ritualistic buildings are perhaps the most stubborn and are subject to the widest range of subtle or wholeheartedly expressionistic interpretation. The articulation of parts becomes a game of rhetoric.

The game of establishing, linking and re-establishing could be considered as analogous to certain forms of poetry or dance. There is the 'line' or sequence, and in order to articulate this line there needs to be a pause, another line or a change in direction; and with the clarification of that line, there is then the need to contribute to a total compositional path, complete with emphasis and de-emphasis. Architectural composition can be seen to follow this strategy exactly.

In a state of advanced technology there is an extremely wide interchange of information and knowledge of precedent. We are culturally challenged by all this. It is surely not enough to be satisfied with the mere notion of buildings made up of predictable elements, strung together by predictable linkages which merely invoke a series of minor linear acknowledgements as surface 'chatter'.

Richards Medical Research Building, Louis I Kahn, Philadelphia, 1958-60

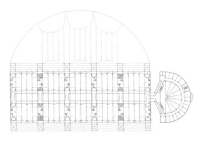

Lyon School of Architecture, Françoise Jourda and Gilles Perroudin, 1982

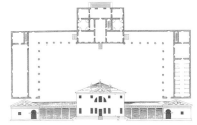

Zeno Villa, Andrea Palladio, 1570

Revolutionary notions – such as that of the city as a single building, a fully serviced landscape with all user-types attached to it at wide intervals, a universal dome/shed/tent/cocoon that is then infiltrated by appropriate devices or a basic 'core' of heat/service equipment that can acquire literally 'any' architectural clothing – all appear to bypass the ponderousness or well-mannered character of normal typologies and their niceties.

Certain architects enjoy games in this area, too. There are ways in which a very large block of building can be presented to the world as a series of buildings. There are ways in which surface familiarity can be used as a form of reassurance that 'all is well'. The hinterland of a calm and apparently benign piece of five-storey neo-Georgian or neo-Bismarck can be a profound, throbbing ten-storey enterprise. Buildings in which the architecture is designed quite intensely, with evaluation of the function, the consistency of functional recognition and the clarity of signal-sending certainly have the moral high ground. Whether this makes them intrinsically 'better' is impossible to argue, but they certainly help the visitor's understanding of them.

We are in a world where services, technical apparatus, controlled manufacture and the conditions of 'scatter' so far described are all directing the commercial and institutional building types towards a wonderful ubiquity. The result is conceptually closer to a scrambled egg than a daintily set meal. Individual components and functional elements are scrambled together in a general 'facility'. The skill of 'joining' is replaced by the inverse skill of 'demarcation'. The tendency runs away from physical articulation and recognisability of types towards a 'wholeness' which brings with it the fear of aesthetic blandness.

If the signals are flattened, then alternative signalling systems may have to be incorporated. Internal partitions and internal routes will need to develop more sophisticated means of identification than colour-coding or super-graphics. Some of those facilities which are ubiquitously available will need to be tuned up to new levels; artificial light blending imperceptibly with daylight; virtual reality blending with reality; electrics and electronics taking over from the familiar language of doorways, separate blocks and hierarchical edifices.

Housing, Ricardo Bofill, Barcelona, 1975

Warehouses, Harald Krogh Stabell, Alesund, Norway, 1906

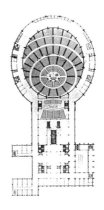

Theatre, Vesnin brothers, 1923 (competition plan)

Consistency

There are few designers who directly encourage a mixture of mannerisms in a single building. The moralities (or habits) that suggest that once you have chosen a language, you should stick with it, are lost in the history of architecture, but are to be found in sufficient parallel art forms to place them in the virtually religious category. Only in Lucien Kroll's Residence Universitaire Catholique du Louvain (1970-77), do we see a deliberate attitude towards the manneristic 'scrambling' of the pieces – in the tradition of *bricolage* – so that the whole thing takes on the air of a randomly growing organism. The theoretical position of the building supports this – a reaction to the tightness of most university buildings and the social or political rigidity that attends them. In a house by Kasahiro Ushi near Tokyo, more than fifty different windows are viewed as both a piece of expressionistic *joie de vivre* and a gesture towards the tedium of consistency that is usual in the choice of windows.

If we design a building that needs or wants to be free from the strictures of formal consistency, we can easily draw from three thousand years of buildings and we can doodle on the drawing board (technically, almost any shape can be constructed). There will, however, be an immediate cry of 'foul' from the articulate onlookers – both architects and laymen – for it will be regarded as a cultural affront as well as a stylistic aberration. At a more subtle level, there are similar strictures that are applied to spatial consistency and inconsistency. There are more let-outs however; function can be invoked for the positioning of windows to help distribute the light, resulting in a rhythm of window-to-wall; the continuous wall itself acts as a further regulator; the release of strictures is allowable for reception spaces, definite appendages (such as conservatories), lecture theatres or towers. These are likely to have their own distinctive form, but may have a rhythmic system that has been reintroduced within themselves.

Organic consistency is even more subtle an issue than spatial consistency. The substance of the building is the first test; the contiguity of surface, the equivalence of weight, the ability to run your eye along the surface without shocking occurrences, the similarity of openings and the similarity of protuberances, balconies, buttresses, fins and antennae. Though they may at first shock, mark or intrigue, these features also seem to have an obligation to belong to the same family as each other on the same building.

The business of 'joining' is then intriguing. The protuberances or main features have a certain obligation to announce themselves and few architects or commentators seem to like a 'puddingy' or ambiguous manner. But they also have the task of contributing to the general ensemble. Thus, they may have to act as reciprocal elements to each other, the corner devices echoed in the re-entry devices where the roof-edge characteristics are reminiscent of the ground-edge characteristics and the openings for entry detailed similarly to the windows. The surface of the walls acts as some kind of binary condition and has to draw lines of connection between these more articulate features. By doing so, attention is drawn to the way in which pieces of building 'sit'.

How does the total building 'sit' on the ground, or in its site? How does the roof sit on the walls and the windows sit into them? How does the bridge sit into the receiving mass of wall, the canopy sit into the front facade and the tall, thin block sit onto its fatter base block? Then, at a much more local scale, how does the window sill sit into the opening and the flying diagonal brace sit onto its bracket? The question, in every case, is to be answered in part by a discussion of its aesthetics but behind that there lies an implicit question of statics, not dissimilar to the way in which weight and poise can be applied to a piece of dance or photography. From this point onwards, we can return to the central issue of 'joining'. In the largest scales of composition, balance and weight, poise and articulation are all related.

Sub-systems

As the complexity of the structure builds up, there is some room for deviation, or apparent deviation. What is probably happening is that sub-systems are being encouraged by their designer. The workshop block, for example, will have its own sets of tolerances and physical loadings or the administration block, its own niceties and demands (maybe from the clients, who will be in this block, but maybe from the architect who suspects that he has the mandate and budget to show off). The canteen block will have its own scale and light quality and the window openings or glass flanks will differ reasonably in each. Yet there will be some remnant of the instinct of consistency. From this point onwards, messages are being sent out from different directions and overlaid. Conceptually, more of a 'plaid' than an even 'weave'. Organically, a subsumed battle; aesthetically, demanding a deft understanding of scale and the capacity for both reading the signals and preventing an overload.

If the workshop block is kept as near to being a miniature factory, the administration block a virtual *palazzo* and the canteen block, a pavilion, those involved may be happy, but the aesthetics, chaotic. The junctions may well be of the 'flash gap' variety, where the surface and the bulk are reduced in the small space between two powerful elements.

Another syndrome lies with the private worlds that are tolerated in certain cities. This may be difficult in villages, the American Midwest, a frontier situation or the desert, yet highly likely in historically self-assured societies where introverted buildings have an intensification of mannerisms but care little for the business of interaction with other buildings. Oxford Colleges, for example, concern themselves with the satisfaction of providing rooms, hall and chapel, along with an entrance condition or lodge. They are inward-looking and may even be developed over intervals of two or more centuries, and consistency of the parts is an implicit consistency of architectonic space rather than a detail. Such a tradition has proved extremely puzzling to all but the most sensitive or brilliant designers. In another way, the Berlin factories of the nineteenth and early twentieth century have a code of subtle deviation from court to court yet an overriding impression of endless repetition. The kasbahs of Africa overlay an implicit discipline with games

Space Museum, Frank O Gehry, Los Angeles, California, 1982

House, Lars Sonck, Helsinki, 1900 (detail)

Offices, Eric Owen Moss, Culver City, California, 1988-90

Gatehouse, Suffolk, c1800

Right Away Ready Mix 2, Holt, Hinshaw, Pfau and Jones, 1987

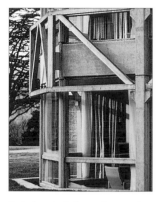

*St Anthony's College, Alison and
Peter Smithson, Oxford, 1979*

*City Hall, Arnstein Arneberg and Magnus
Paulsson, Oslo, 1918-47*

Shops and apartments, Tel Aviv, c1938

Mathildenhöhe, JM Olbrich, Darmstadt, 1907

*Hotels and apartments on Brighton seafront,
nineteenth and twentieth century*

of subtle variation and insertion. Japanese cities too, have an intrinsic quality of implosion within apparently straightforward repeated typologies, eventually leading to exquisite surprise. The lanes are full of objects, but are clearly formulaic. Because of the price of land, the houses are unable to play any major organisational tricks, yet the process is one of stage-by-stage unravelling. The ability of the formal tradition to span from large buildings down to the layout of food in a lunch-box repeatedly creates an ever-available progression within.

Scattering

As a precedent we have the village, but there are many other instances of the scattered yet related community. In recent years it has become something of a social gesture to present a community of interest (such as a company headquarters or a hospital) as a series of buildings, each complete physically but related by routes, paths and services. There has been antipathy to the large block in the green field and so the field is apparently more acceptably peppered with pieces of that block. This presupposes that a fairly passive role be played by the individual parts. However, this is not traditionally the case.

The fragmented complex can contain a plethora of self-consciously defined buildings; 'pavilions', 'markers', exposed flanks and terraces. 'Quotations' from the main building can be sent out into the space available and, if aligned carefully, make quite sure that their quotational relevance can be picked up by any intelligent observer. A key role in this syndrome will be played by paths, or possibly by embankments and vistas. These will have more to do with the overriding geometry of the whole complex than the small, inserted buildings. In this case, therefore, the joining element is not a building but a device of different substance and different form, the role of which is that of a 'joiner'.

Consciously or unconsciously, there are now some buildings that attempt a version of this tactic, whilst at the same time preserving the integrity of the covered surface. The trick with such buildings is to load the linking elements (probably corridors, colonnades, trellises or wings) with timber strips leading to tough brick bulks, and thin steel and glass spindles running between heroic

Novarro House, Lloyd Wright, Hollywood, 1930

Housing, Klaus Kada, Graz, 1989

Santa Colomna de Cervelló Caves, Antonio Gaudi, 1898-1915

pavilions. The 'tree' analogy is too obvious to deny such an organisation.

In a sense, the determinism of all this as seemingly inevitable built logic or as a built diagram causes some designers to shy away. The idea of the 'non-building-building' becomes highly, if romantically, attractive. This might be a series of removable parts, such as trucks which are generally expendable, exchangeable, and demand major modification over a short span of time. Alternatively, it might be successfully unidentifiable to the point of seeming as if it were never there at all. The underground building is one such case – although it sets up a myriad of additional architectural problems of identity and articulation of its own. The non-building-building may be hidden from view, pretending to be just a wall, an embankment, just part of something else. In the end, however, placement will bring in its own demands for identity, definition and conditions of joining elements.

A final discussion of 'joining' runs towards a more cultural territory. We are not now talking of the techniques or even the niceties; we are talking about architecture *per se*. We are observing the fact that buildings do send messages to each other, or rather, that the literature and gossip of an age enable one building to repeat, quote in part, distance from and contradict the characteristics of another. Even buildings with a minimum of rhetoric do this. The accelerated state of publishing, photography and other communications lead to this exchange existing between continents and racing through a culture within two or three years. In this book, I will myself be identifying my own set of seminal buildings; these, or others, then become part of the public domain and, as such, are up for grabs. So, if these sets of corresponding buildings were part of some actual located complex, they are there for the connoisseur and are ready to be joined and dissected in the mind, in a speedy manner if compared with the eighteenth century when the traveller's notebook had to suffice. The real trick for the designer is the ability to look at what is in the immediate foreground – on the board, screen or through the window – and simultaneously project towards, engage with and reject the 'corresponding' building with which he is in dialogue. To succeed at the business of joining, is to know when to detach.

Karlsplatz Station, Otto Wagner, Vienna, 1888-89

Hestercombe, Edwin Lutyens and Gertrude Jekyll, Somerset, 1900

Hedge-House, West Palm Beach, Florida

STRUCTURES

*Rheinhalle, Wilhelm Kreis, 1927,
diagram of the structure and
exterior by Riepart and Dahl*

Homogeneity or Poised Disintegrity?

When you are considering structures you need to force your mind into a greater state of discrimination than usual, and perhaps look back beyond architectural history to the first real structures that were reinterpretations of the cave: stone, grass, sticks or blocks of ice piled up as a homogeneous mass creating a hollow chamber. A fundamental shift, however, occurred when there seemed to be more than one material to choose from. In a region with both stones and trees there would be a choice, resulting in deliberation over the components of castles, cottages, barns, walled villages. Thus, the discovery of the issue of weight as against cover (involving the likelihood of collapse) established a theory of structures.

The extent to which the subsequent development has been led by function, opportunity or 'dare' reminds us of earlier discussions. Function demanded an ever-increasing number of gambits: long spaces, high spaces and repeated spaces. The structural implications of all these became clear. Opportunity occurred when some bright person noted that large arches can combine to deal with even larger spaces, when lighter loads at the top of a building are compensated for by more daylight (also finding that the heavy structure at the base is the ideal place for cooling wine or cooling-down prisoners). 'Dare' is the more difficult of the three motivations to discuss. It is one of those origins of professionalism in which the guy with the knowledge enjoys 'showing off'. It is also the most fascinating of the three developments and is probably the underlying theme of this chapter. We only dimly care to know of all the collapsed arches, dangerously thin walls or flimsy bridges and can only occasionally trace the sequence by which a barn or a church has been successively propped up by larger and larger buttresses. The positive side of the argument suggests that a very major part of architectural endeavour rests with the continued existence of designers who have not been deterred or dismayed by these mishaps and consequently strive to push materials and techniques to ever-further limits in order to create space.

I have deliberately referred to those involved as 'designers' knowing that it is common to discuss structure as being the province of engineering just as it is normal (and legally advisable) for us to work together with structural engineers.

Galerie des Machines, *Ferdinand Dutert,*
Paris, 1886-89 (demolished 1910)

Sports hall, Christoph Langhof and Peter Rice,
Berlin, 1990 (roof detail)

Illustration from '101 Fantasies', Jacob
Chernikhov, 1928

It has become a matter of architectural politics to take a view on the integrity or disintegrity of the formal process together with the 'engineering'. Throughout the nineteenth century in particular, there were conspicuous examples of the engineer shaping the shed, bridge or factory and the architect being employed to give it a 'face'. Some contemporary architects find this quite satisfactory. To others this is a tragic assault on the process of design, the integrity of all the issues involved being central. After all, engineering 'honesty' claimed to be a pivot of twentieth-century Modernism with the formal language of more experimental buildings deriving so much from structural ideas that disintegrity seems to some of us like advocating 'limblessness'.

In the intellectually uncluttered times of the cottage and barn, the relative merits of different varieties of timber or stone must have emerged as soon as travel became extensive. If early buildings remained fairly 'total' in form (with a resulting sigh of relief as soon as the weather could be kept out) ambition mixed with intelligent observation began to overlay this with the experience of a widening range of materials. More activities prompt the making of wider and wider openings in walls. Roof timbers start to allow for openings and protuberances. If we look at castles and the edges of town walls or farm walls we become aware of one of the most enduring tactics of structure; the setting up of a tough, solid spine providing a basis for all kinds of weaker, lighter and subordinate structures to lean onto it. This strategy persists through to today as an attractive idea and it is admirably catered for by the technology of concrete – for the spine – and an ever increasing number of technologies for the lightweight suppliants.

Since castles and other defended territories had to withstand violation, there emerged the idea of a variable structure. If we add to that the idea of conscious 'under-design' that must have come from the making of military camps and the settlements of wandering tribes we have a whole range of available measurement, stressing and discrimination. Since that time, structure has no longer been a question of a single set of circumstances but has been subject to opinion and need. Obviousness becomes enmeshed with traditions of practice. Extreme design becomes the product of stressed circumstance as well as expertise.

Of course, such a comfortable relationship cannot suffice. Design issues were generated by the need to make bridges, towers, tunnels, viaducts and very large roofed spaces. To deal with the continual stretching involved, a greater and greater range of typologies and techniques are added. Ways of thickening, bracing, propping or spanning from point to point are incorporated. Much of our 'first principles of structure' thinking stems from this tradition of development, but it is essential constantly to look beyond the immediate line of tradition. One could even suggest that if designing a cottage, it might still be appropriate to recall all the available gambits of bridge-building. If designing a bridge, it might just be worth considering our accumulated experience of roof types.

The central paradox lies thus, that it is foolish and tiresome to attempt to skin and span a space without a clear understanding of basic structural principles. At the same time, the opportunity created by the virtuosity of current techniques and materials is allied to the fundamental fact that design need never be restricted to traditional interpretational models. Morally tricky, but logical, is the fact that many of our available techniques have grown up through the endeavours of war and space technology. Alloys, adhesives, fixings, fibres and the hybridisation of metals and plastics have come, more often than not, from outside architecture. We still tend to think in terms of 'wall' and 'roof' despite the conceptual narrowness of a building that is too simply 'layered' in horizontal strips. We still think in terms of standardising the size of beams, rafters, wall openings and wall thicknesses despite knowing that computerised calculation enable the most subtle of profiles.

In the Guggenheim Centre at Bilbao, Frank Gehry has been able to bypass both the tedium and the restriction that would have come from a traditional design process. The audacious and evocative models that are made in his office (and with which he is always personally involved) can be 'tracked' by instruments and the information passed straight into a computer programme that can quantify, profile and componentise the pieces of stone that have to be cut. The tradition of drawing everything and of effectively being restricted by what can be drawn has been broken, so the form and structure can come directly from the idea. It is worth comparing this experience with that of another heroic twentieth-century

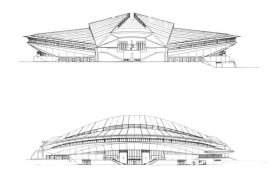

Tokyo Metropolitan Gymnasium, Fumihiko Maki, 1990

Guggenheim Centre, Frank O Gehry, Bilbao, 1992-96

School at Lund, Bengt Erdman, Sweden, 1975

piece, the Sydney Opera House of Jørn Utzon. Here, the formal and structural instincts are clear but the actual process of calculation and computerisation arerendered far longer by the comparative primitiveness of the computer systems available thirty years before the Bilbao work. Both examples succeed, however, in repudiating away the narrowness of 'walls-and-roof' architecture.

The more simple definitions of homogeneity are also becoming suspect. Cynically, we can remember that many of the 'machine aesthetic' buildings of the late 1920s and 1930s were apparently made from a universal white cement blancmange, but when peeled away consist of bizarre combinations of brick, stone, steel and even timber that is then skinned to appear homogeneous. With growing awareness of insulation and cost-weight ratios as well as the disappearance of craft traditions, we are increasingly reliant upon mixtures of technique and the layering-in of prefabricated meshes, links, plastic inserts and flexible fixings. At the moment, these are used circumstantially but aeroplane, car and ship design suggest that a third generation of 'high tech' thinking could evolve: where computer programmes exist to allow us to scramblein a whole series of speculations and combinations of structure and material. Another attack on the over-simplicity of thinking merely in terms of wall, floor and roof, comes from the understanding of the way in which loads and stresses are transferred from place to place in a building. The 'plastic' theory of structures follows this process, rather in the way that we might follow the gathering together of watercourses until their combination in a great river. The results of this method of analysis lead to a far more variegated and fluid combination of parts than by reducing everything to sets of classic elements (such as a separated 'main roof' and regular strips of wall and floor). Instead, force and form creep along the available substance, quite prepared to change direction and profile. Clearly, such analysis aims to be as witty and resourceful as the forces themselves in responding to points of stress, hence it is most appropriate to reinforced concrete construction.

A completely alien approach to this fluidity comes from the idea of the 'cage'. Its origins lie in Classical optimisation. The usefulness of the standard element, be it tree trunk or steel beam. Moreover the admiration of Cartesian geometry appeals to a variety of intellectual positions in architecture. As it develops, however, there emerges a certain delight in the potential of it as but one stage in a progression. For if we have a primary 'cage' or network of repeated structure existing at a sufficiently large scale, we can set up any number of subordinate conditions. Moreover, these do not have to conform to the cage's geometry or aesthetic. There is a parallel with the case of the wall and lean-to. In the case of the cage however, there is an eventual resolution back to the major system. All too often, consideration of it as an option is restricted by the morality of Classical thinking, but it need not be. Certain attempts made to develop cities and high-density housing during the 1960s involved the idea of the 'megastructure' which usually involved a repeatable cage or framework of some sort. Thinking swung away from these models, but structural engineering continued to explore the legitimacy of creating a major matrix that could deal with both the optimal loads as well as eccentric loads. The development of space frames and tower cranes, aided by the continual development of service machinery and plants of all kinds, moved onwards. Now we have the opportunity to lay down 'mats' of major structure into which whole rooms can be inserted. We also have the chance to regard vertical structure less as a 'wall' and more as horizontal 'mats' just described. What now emerges is the option to see structure as a general strategy and differently as a local strategy. Again, this is both a sophistication of traditional thinking and also a less hidebound, more fluid way of looking at design The ability to provide for growth, change and the insertion of extra equipment supports the technique and structuring becomes a dynamic activity.

Another organic model is the agglomerate mass. Few of us can ignore that primitive set of instincts suggested by the sight of a pyramid, ziggurat or any building that can be described as a 'magnificent pile'. Perhaps it is man's romantic wish to reproduce the mountain, a harking back to the magnificent protection of the cave-structure. Conveniently, there are a number of logical ways of piling-up a building that echo the natural flow and intensification of forces towards the ground. The typical section of a cathedral with its high roof and transference of the roof load onto the buttresses (which may include flying buttresses and arching over the aisles onto a lower set of buttresses) is a skeletal version. The domed central space with smaller chambers wrapping around it is a more solid version. The tightly packed city – with an almost continual series of modestly sized rooms bracing themselves between a regular run of vertical cross walls (or 'party' walls) – can be seen as a further example of the agglomerate mass. A way of designing within such conditions is to test out the resilience of the existing structural mass and add in one's own contribution as infill.

Such an attitude towards design is acceptable if it is adopted with intelligence. The structural purist can be forgiven, however, if he is suspicious of those who merely flop around a space, erecting a wall and a beam here, a piece of mass and a flimsy wall there. This type of situation is always resolved by the rather panicked insertion of a small column or an arch, for aesthetic reasons. Perhaps the consciousness of a structural strategy at the first instance accords more naturally with the making of a building of balance, sequence and discrimination, while honing some of the fundamental balances already noted. By analogy, the addition of too many small elements to a basically balanced and logical structure can sound parallel warnings. If the calculations of load and deformation start to suggest that the basic structure will have to be full of 'specials', it may well be that the formal and organisational conditions are out of hand. It is not just a question of taste that states that too many components fight the idea of elegance. Pluralist values in architecture expose the fine line that exists between theoretical 'elegance' of structure – an idea of consequential moves made in the pursuit of a delicate balance of forces – and the allied concept of poised disintegrity.

Three Japanese buildings demonstrate this poised disintegrity as it develops through a recent tradition: Kenzo Tange's Tokyo National Gymnasium of 1964, Fumihiko Maki's Tepia Science Pavilion and, finally, Toyo Ito's Municipal Museum at Yatsoshiro of 1988-91. Tange's building (of reinforced concrete) sets out to establish a central 'tower' element from which major spaces can unwind. This piece of virtuosity is augmented by other pieces of unwrapping. In Maki's building (mainly a steel structure) the unwrapping becomes a developed mannerism in which the exposed surfaces take on a deliberately disintegrative form, though the structural series is very much in control. Ito's work is inherently lighter than that of his elders and at times, the Yatsoshiro building feels as if it is about to fall apart.

On closer inspection however, there is a square-cornered concrete bunker from which various pieces sprout out. There are also conditions in which some regular runs of supported valleys of the roof can run out, but then be sliced off in an irregular fashion. A hull-like vessel sits somewhere above. Ito and Kimura (Ito's structural engineers) reach a point of controlled nonchalance that suggests that a structure can fold, glide or flake away at will.

The Emancipation of Structure

It is my aim to avoid a split in our analysis of the relevance of structure to the design of buildings, between narrowly concentrating upon a line of structural feats on the one hand, or constantly leaving the pure engineering somewhere at the back of the charting of architectural expressionism, as something of a support technique. The more likely story is another case of the inspired push-and-pull of invention and information. Politically, it is clear that some incredible buildings have come about in periods of intense invention and endeavour. The pursuit of wealth and Empire, the battle with the weather, the lateral thought that can leap from shipbuilding, dam building or manufacture has naturally stimulated inventive architecture. It is obvious that wealthy societies were able to take the risk of innovation in the first instance, but with the accumulation of knowledge that we now have, the results are available to be source material for 'local' mutations. More than this, there is a shift of attitude towards skilfully engineered structures, knowing that they can often result in a better and therefore cheaper solution to a problem than that of the 'walls-and-roof' approach.

To remind ourselves that the relevance of structure has been at the centre of architectural debate for more than a century we must remember that Viollet-le-Duc's *Annales archéologiques* were published in 1854-68. This work advocated the centrality of the development of efficiency and economy, and traced this search through to the Gothic cathedrals of the thirteenth century. Moreover, it was proposed that this be a point of departure for architects in the nineteenth century and, consequently, the *Annales* became enmeshed in the mid-century battle between Classicists and Goths but was certainly underpinned from another direction – the British tradition of quizzical and inventive engineering which was often based on the idea of 'dare'; seeing just how far a piece of structure can thrust, twist or hang before it collapses, and poising the formation just so. The first cast-iron bridge was erected at Coalbrookdale in 1779 and from this point onwards the history of architecture is intertwined with the use of iron – and subsequently steel – in its continued process of creating structured space.

Warehouses became framed in iron but encased in brickwork, thus formalising the practice of reinforcing masonry that had started in the thirteenth century. However, it is in its more expansive mode that we realise the fantastic abilities of iron and steel as a material that can be extruded with tremendous control, by the accuracy of manufacture, as well as very precise jointing. The resulting profiles, networks, trusses, lace works and complex configurations of all types make it possible to make an enclosure which is unprecedentedly thin, with the ability to let in light and yet have great strength. The development of structure has moved to a definitively emancipated position furthest from the ancient sheltering pile.

Three London buildings of the nineteenth century illustrate the heroism of the iron-framed shed. At King's Cross Station the tough brick front prepares for an equally sparse but brilliantly tuned shed. The Palm House at Kew Gardens is a complete iron and glass envelope with the necessary climate created by heat being drawn up from the cellar via carefully placed vents. At once formal but direct, its central space is flanked by two arms of almost Futurist aesthetic and the cross section is brilliantly direct as a piece of structuring. The skins of the upper and lower areas are formed from arcs of very slim ironwork filled with thin, lapped pieces of glass. Thus structural form and enveloping form run delicately close together and the design by John Turner and Decimus Burton remains one of the great icons of the machine aesthetic. Isambard Kingdom Brunel was the designer of the shed of Paddington Station. Already famed for his bridges, tunnels and other station buildings, he displays a virtuosity that can absorb intersecting transepts, a shift of direction at the south-eastern corner and the most developed lace work of arches that has not subsequently been superseded.

The increased insistence upon fire protection combined with the need for a well-trained workforce has kept the development of the steel frame as the preferred structure of more sophisticated countries, so the history of the last hundred years has perhaps been dominated by the many attractions of reinforced concrete. An irony exists in the fact that steel is a critical component of the latter, but it is the apparent plasticity, homogeneity and substantiality of concrete that makes it attractive. Add to this the fact that it can be manipulated by a relatively unsophisticated

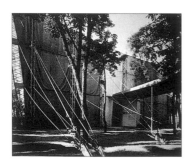

Temps Nouveau Exhibition Pavilion, Le Corbusier, Paris, 1937

Paddington Station, Isambard Kingdom Brunel and MD Wyatt, London, 1852-54

Palm House, John Turner and Decimus Burton, Kew Gardens, London, 1851

workforce and easily transported, and you have a strong rival to steel.

The Charles VI Mill at Tourcoing by François Hennebique was constructed in 1895 with the concrete structure clearly exposed. By 1897 the Church of St Jean de Montmartre in Paris by Anatole de Baudot existed with a clear, even rhetorical, display of concrete form. Though concrete had already been used as an infill material, these buildings mark the arrival of a critically vital manner in which to deal with structure. The implication runs on from the idea of plastic structure so that with a concrete system (whether frame, shell, hulk or any hybrid form) the material is continuous. Concrete can also be absorbed into brick, stone or panelled walling so that the 'drama' of structure is eschewed. Having reached this point of temerity, it is time to return to a more inspired moment.

In Robert Maillart's work, the inherited principle of separating the functions of bearing and loading is bypassed. All the parts of his later bridges are integral. Folding and curving the solids as demanded by the forces within it, he incorporates elements such as the road itself that would traditionally be treated as a separate element. He tailors the fins according to the specific needs – rather than maintaining a common set of profiles and dimensions. In a much more formalised way, Auguste Perret develops the notion of reinforced concrete as both structure and total form in his work (with an aesthetic that could come from no other material) the key instance being his church of Notre Dame du Raincy of 1922-23. The definitive moment for this material is not, however, reached until the emergence of Pier Luigi Nervi (1891-1979) who was able to knead it into such virtuoso fluidity of form and total control of space that one is forced to admit that structure itself can create a total architectural statement. In other words, by the late 1940s – by which time Nervi had built the Communal Stadium of Florence (1930-32) and the Exhibition Building of Turin (1948-49) – structure had become emancipated, with steel-framed or reinforced concrete structures having the potential to span very large distances, to release all surfaces for the admission of light, to leap, twist, carry immense loads in as straightforward or as expressionistic a way imaginable and even all in the same building, if required!

The childhood cry, 'Look! No hands!', was appropriate to many buildings of the 1950s where a carefree and unashamedly demonstrative gesture of structural acrobatics is performed. In Italy, Brazil or anywhere that felt the need for a flamboyant statement, concrete legs and arms, exotic shells or steel peacocks were possible. The instincts were twofold: to demonstrate a belief in the future by way of the extreme rhetoric of technology and to demonstrate that a new public architecture had been discovered, that matched anything from the Renaissance or the nineteenth century. Meanwhile, engineering itself had developed into a mode that continues today; where the heroic feats of size, span and shape are conceptually exceeded by the abilities of new materials and the perfection of our handling of the old materials. An intelligent approach to the design of a structure must refer to the state of the art in terms of materials and expertise available at the site. This approach must also handle the increasing overlap between technologies and the erosion of old taboos. Structural glass is no longer an eccentricity, neither are windows as a heat source, structural columns as fire hydrants, roofs as gardens, suspended structures as artificial ground, wall panels that can deflect with the wind, buildings that roll and whole pieces of structure that can disappear and reappear.

Structure is linked historically with so-called 'technology'. Of course, all building activity is some sort of technology, even the most primitive, but in recent years there has been a conscious espousal of technical apparatus and exposed structural devices under the name 'High Tech'. Buildings that come within this category are often well within the known technical limits of steel work or suspended structural design, but the fact that they celebrate their use of structural techniques and manufactured components in a gleeful way makes them also part of this state of emancipation. English and French buildings of the 1970s to 1990s seem to celebrate this more enthusiastically than any others; not perhaps surprising if we remember the key role that these two countries played in the development of engineering theory and the invention of engineered elements. The almost athletic character of a structure can be used to identify the best High Tech architecture and we should be able to identify the acts of 'hanging', 'leaping', 'skinning', 'gliding', 'threading', 'breathing', 'swinging', 'billowing', and note their ability to be 'gossamer thin', 'seamless', 'machine made' and even, in some cases, 'un-architectural'. Philosophically, this last intention is the manifestation of a desire for design to be as inevitable and functionally logical as that of an aeroplane design, a turbine or a ship. That it should be analogous to industrial design and formally inevitable is still an unlikely reality. Such wishes do, however, give certain designers a preference for establishing a highly particularised structural icon at the outset, whereby the rest of the design remains subordinate; the dream being that, in this way, the inevitable has been established.

The results can be insensitive, cranky or (sometimes) wonderful. Piano and Rogers' Centre Pompidou, Norman Foster's Ipswich offices and Jean Nouvel's Arab World Institute in Paris are total structures which demonstrate unfettered optimism and unabashed belief in technology. As structural typologies, however, they are quite modest.

Palm House, Volcker Giencke, Graz, 1991-95

Sydney Opera House, Jørn Utzon, 1956-73 (detail)

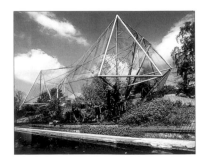

Aviary at London Zoo, Cedric Price, Frank Newby and Lord Snowdon, 1970

Primary Elements

Without prejudice to any particular technique, the design of a total structure has a certain logic. If we can deal with the whole body in one mannerism, we shall have a coherent object that is identifiable, manageable and powerful. As we have discussed already, certain architects will prefer totality from the point of view of rhetoric. Structurally, there will be less 'bother' with a single body. Its roof will have a standard condition that must bring itself down and round the body. Perhaps it will even be *of* the body. We can return to the Tange sports hall and the Nervi building to find such a body or to Konrad Wachsmann's Cellular Construction System of 1950-53. Naturally such totality is appropriate to a hall or hangar, but recent commercial exploitation of the 'shed' again raises the question of whether we are treating this typology as a serious generic type.

The great railway sheds of the nineteenth century had no fear in the making of a total statement. The abilities of steel and concrete construction are now extended beyond the wildest dreams of their support. There is the potential for the 'body' building to be totally integral, with light-admitting, environment-sealing, heating-integral facilities. The Buckminster Fuller geodesic dome hints at a total aesthetic. Other models are, therefore, surely possible.

If primacy is not necessarily totality, then we can look at it as the 'triggering' condition for a developed sequence of structural ideas. If roof and main carcass remain separate, there will still be the essential 'ring' of impact. The components of the roof and their regularity will land upon a wall or a series of vertical supports. If so developed, the response to this impact is quite cavalier, but common sense suggests that the piece of structure descending diagonally is in line with the vertical piece of structure, ready to receive its force. Special interferences with this may cause interesting deviations, but this state of 'roof and ring' is so basic and logical that there is generally no need to avoid it. Already we have an expressionistic choice: we may want to express the progress of the structure falling towards the ground with a consequent 'vertical' bias. If we want the main wall to have visual primacy, however, we may suppress this. One way is to emphasise the significance of the top of the wall. The condition

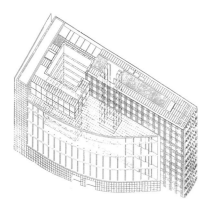

Arab World Institute, Jean Nouvel, Paris, 1981

Endless House, Frederick Kiesler, 1923-60 (model)

Great Yarmouth Pier Pavilion, JR Cockrill, c1912

83

that I call 'ring' is critical here. My implication is that it is conceptually analogous to a hem in a dress, a plate in a meal, a seat edge in a chair. This is the moment at which both the falling and binding conditions of the structure are coincident. However, they share a lateral commonality, hence my term 'ring'.

Classical architecture made great play of this condition – so much so that it is synonymous with the cornice. Classical architecture also made great play of the skeletal element of column – even in its semi-suppressed version of pilaster. A primary structure is often a skeletal cage, the verticals of the cage visible to all. The human skeleton is not, however, all backbone and ribs, and analogies of the head, arms, etc, are to be found in more complex buildings. Remaining somewhat humanoid, we can look at the spine as a key generator of structure. Where ceremony is not involved, a central row of columns or a spine wall is a highly satisfactory way of generating a built form. This spine can be formed by a corridor and we then have a brilliantly forceful generator, the spine being the route, the operational generator and also the focus of the structure from which all other parts of the system develop. Stretch the diagram and you have the Gothic nave.

Much of this presumes that our building is based upon vertical walls, which may not be so, or, more interestingly, may not depend upon vertical resolution of forces. It may be that the loads coming down are being transferred diagonally, vertically and even transferred diagonally across from one zone to the next in plan (the operational floors and walls need not be part of the structural system, after all). A primary system is probably definable as one in which a perfectly complete and aesthetically satisfying structure could be placed in space. Demanding no further parts and infinitely interpretable, such a definition suggests that a primary structure is a matter of principle, balance and logical sequence. This in turn suggests that such issues of scale, aesthetic detail, surface and the like, have no particular significance. An interesting return, for a moment, to the issue of the abstractness (or lack of 'architecturalness') of structural issues?

The twentieth century has been prolific in its creation of total objects, especially domes, sheds and buildings resembling 'landed objects' with a complete presence in themselves. Many of these are 'skin' structures, either of shell concrete or an

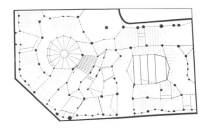

Casa Milà, Antonio Gaudi, Barcelona, 1906-10

Morrow Branch Library, Scogin Elam and Bray, Morrow, Georgia, 1991

Paramount Laundry Redevelopment, Eric Owen Moss, Culver City, California, 1989

inflatable skin. Many steel or aluminium structures are essentially similar in concept, a series of small-scale components combined to form some form of 'mat' that structures the outer skin. The ability of adhesives and sophisticated fixings to extend the range of timber structures has now reached such versatility that many 'skin type' structures can be similarly formed. Once again, the clarity of the system may well be found in the ubiquitous nature of its components. The idea of a construction 'system' tends to be the butt of architectural intellectual politics; the 'system' advocates being regarded as rather boring and technocratic by the advocates of bespoke design. In reverse, the former often feel a certain religiosity towards the search for the perfect system. In identifying primary structure, I am less interested in this battle than in reminding the designer that an overview and a sequence of moves is just common sense.

Secondary Elements

The thrust of a structure established, there are the positions of the key structural elements to determine. Placing many series of columns close together can create an atmosphere reminiscent of a forest. The alternative, of placing as few column points as possible, will result in those columns that do exist exerting a strong, perhaps overbearing, visual emphasis. The designer may wish to establish a structural line that can be 'read', but then set up a counterpoint of another weight acting around it. To have lines of glazing interweaving or deliberately avoiding lines of columns is a familiar gambit.

The impact of a roof or ceiling structure has some parallels. It is generally assumed that a relatively small-scale ceiling element repeated many times, will establish identity, but no more. The onlooker may nonetheless find the resulting insistence of repeat form quite irritating, as in the case of many coffered or trussed ceilings. My definitions are aesthetic or atmospheric since it is possible to engineer almost any ceiling or roof configuration; the rest is either laziness or aesthetics. The choice of secondary elements is often far harder than that of the primary structure because of this expressionistic factor.

The hope is that an inevitability can be suggested to the second series of design decisions. That a certain span of roof and interval of support can suggest two or three obvious types of truss, beam or spread load (such as a space frame or a coffered structure) will need to be 'held' in the mind an assessment and the aesthetic impact of the various alternatives must be made, with the criteria being those of the rest of the building. Is it a highly rhetorical building with a rhetorical structure? Is the structure to be the muted element? Is the aim to be skeletal, massive, directional or non-directional? Is the aim for lightness or for a certain emphasis of presence that may contrast with another part of the building? Is the roof to be 'read' as one or do we want the interval of the elements to be staccato, busy, cosy or symbolic of technicality? I am suggesting that this stage of the design is realised through the choice of a structural expressionism. It is likely to be the columns and beams (or their equivalents) that are felt, appreciated, identified on all the drawings, and that stand out in the photographs of the built object.

Arguably, the first set of decisions should be the determinants of all these. Reality suggests, though, that the secondary parts are the strongest in effect.

Systematically, the choice of direction will have been made, but interval will matter greatly. When the whole thing is built, the visual effect of depth and thickness cannot be over-emphasised. Whatever we say about the universality of structural principles and the enduring appropriateness of parts (the most likely giveaways of tradition), technique or culture are also going to emanate from the qualities of these key secondary parts. Just as in the deep past, the identification of a historical moment came from looking at the depth of a window recess or the fineness of its tracery. The idiosyncrasies of beam thickness, column tapering, panel emphasising, or simply the crumbliness of the concrete cover will speak eloquently to the connoisseur.

Tertiary Elements

If the temptations and frustrations of 'secondary' design have been navigated, the last phase can seem to be a matter of creative light relief. A trap of course. In many countries it is normal for the architect to abdicate from the design of anything more intricate than that which can be drawn to a scale of 1:100 or maybe 1:50. The assumption is that the common local techniques can deal with most conditions and even allow for the incorporation of components that may well have been developed through exhaustive stages of technical development. A similarly thorough process made by the architect may be considered as time-wasting and expensive. However, few really great buildings have emerged from such a process. A close look at the mannerisms of significant designers will reveal their obsessiveness concerning the choice of parts. The turning of corners, the connecting of two pieces of metal, the shadow of a sunbeam passing through an aperture in the concrete – mannerism or integrity, this is the stuff of design.

Once again, the procedure of dealing with each problem as it comes along and produces a hundred solutions to twenty conditions might be relaxed as an approach, but it is more likely to be weak-willed. At the detail level we are faced with a dilemma. The most direct way of roofing a series of small rooms may be

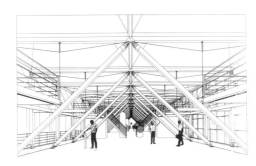

Lyon School of Architecture, Françoise Jourda and Gilles Perroudin, Lyon, 1982

Lyon School of Architecture, Françoise Jourda and Gilles Perroudin, Lyon, 1982

Apartments, NC House, Itsuko Hasegawa, Tokyo, 1984

to construct a simple concrete slab. The most direct way of making a pedestrian ramp may be to support it with a row of modest columns. The rest of the building may, however, be on a far more generous scale: a thin slab and a fussy run of columns might destroy the directness of the ensemble, so the slab will be replaced by a series of overscaled trusses and the ramp interpreted as a structural beam that can leap upwards in one go. In parallel situations, there would be architects who want to relate everything to a 3 metre grid, for example, thus relating even the major spaces to this articulated dimension and calculating the structural system back to that measure, whatever first principles might suggest.

High Tech buildings have an advantage here, since their detail parts are usually of the same material (probably steel or aluminium) and the diminutive elements have a direct similarity of type and manufacture to the large elements. One is often visually attracted to the 'pieces' and their jointing. Some structural engineers have argued that so-called High Tech is more a means of stylisation than a definitively technical way of dealing with a structure, in other words, a form of 'showing off'. Yet surely the Classical and High Gothic of the mannerisms were equally a form of 'showing off'. The celebration of the column and its bedding in towards the ground (marked by a series of elaborate mouldings and pads or the Gothic window tracery) made sure you appreciated the cleverness with which glass could be accommodated. High Tech is in a great tradition. A historical view will, however, recognise the signs that this is a style waiting at the point of departure, as did Classicism and the Gothic. Establishing some recognisable elements that refer directly to structure and construction are likely (as were its predecessors) to be debased, softened, overlaid, but never quite lost.

I am suggesting that the designer of a building, having negotiated the first and second tiers of structural overview, analysis and, then, choice, will need to be clear about language in sustaining the details. Certain objects that appear to be structural elements can actually be appendages or, rather, extra to the basic building object. Returning to the nineteenth century, the casual observer of the chocolate factory at Noisiel-sur-Marne, built between 1871 and 1872 by Jules Saulnier, might be forgiven for enjoying the diagonal embroidery of iron straps

Lawyer's offices, Co-op Himmelb(l)au, Vienna, 1989 (interior)

Chocolate Factory, Jules Saulnier, Noisiel-sur-Marne, 1871-72

Sports hall, Enric Miralles, Huesca, completed 1993

87

that complete an apparent tapestry work with the brickwork patterning and the small-paned windows. These straps are, however, but part of an elaborate system of brick vaults that sit into wrought-iron joists which are then carried by external lattice girders and internal columns. The brickwork is a mere veneer so that the 'embroidery' is in reality a major part of the structural system rather than the 'wall'.

Though we started the structural discussion at the level of basics (the shed, the dome, the cage, the spine wall, the tower) and these are still to be considered at the outset, there is a contrary approach. This will first of all appraise the whole range of likely conditions and configurations, attempt to find some co-ordinates and then devise a series of structural moves that can 'descend' upon space. The result may unashamedly switch from load-bearing to suspended structure, from close-knit columns to wide spans – structure as part of a cultural supermarket.

Experimental Structures

The mixture of empiricism and circumstantial logic that has just been described does, nonetheless, have a certain flatness about it. Structures are surely for heroes? Some of the most fantastic structures exist today as part of the aircraft industry, the pop music industry or even at the end of your street where a very deft hydraulic arm is about to grab a piece of equipment out of someone's back yard. Magical exploits of discovery in the fields of microtechnology, genetics, crystallography and electronics are as heroic as anything from the nineteenth century, except that many of them are minute and few of them result in large public objects. The building as such is therefore threatened with a certain generic archaism along with old ships, steam trains and typewriters. Unless, of course, it can be the umbrella concept for all collections of artefact and equipment that make life more comfortable.

High Tech has already borrowed from ships and aeroplanes for many of its bits and pieces. The plastics industry was originally associated with the domestic scale of appliances and household items, but has now become indispensable for the production of drainage components and insulation. At a more generic level, the possibilities of variable plastic components inspire the most advanced engineers.

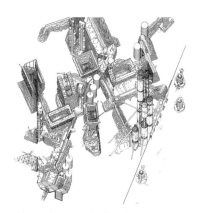

Plug- in City, Peter Cook, 1964

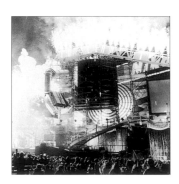

Steel Wheels for the 1989 Rolling Stones tour, Mark Fisher and Jonathan Park

The Diplomatic Club, Frei Otto, Riyadh, 1983

The ability of cells to be grown and 'nano' technology can now produce a built surface that can virtually mutate. The 'grown' building is within our grasp.

The idea of the removable and replaceable building has inspired many of us since the 1960s. My own 'Plug-in City' of 1964-65 presented a series of structures together, some of giant dimension (able to contain lifts and drains) and some only structured for their own purposes (plastic or metal living capsules). There were also moveable gantries and inflatable enclosures. The ecology movement of the 1970s reacted away from such an apparently 'consumerist' direction, but more and more of the ideas have become absorbed by the architectural mainstream. We have virtual megastructures in the street and infrastructure systems of a city such as Tokyo and there are more and more componented building elements, many of which are designed for replacement.

Inflatable structures have slowed down in popularity, but, along with the electric car, they exist as one of the 'sleepers' of technology, in fact waiting for better materials and a new generation of advocacy. The combination of time with form and impact exists most creatively in the world of rock concerts and it is no coincidence that Mark Fisher – a key architect in this field – was one of the pioneers of the second generation of inflatable structure development (out of the 'big bag' period and into the tuneable, sculptural mode). The Rolling Stones' *Steel Wheels* assemblage and Roger Waters' *The Wall* both combinen large demountable steel structures with a certain critique of the High Tech world (already the beginning of the 1990s). Together with his then partner, the engineer Jonathan Park, Fisher created a set that disappeared in an explosion of flames, only to reappear mysteriously at the beginning of the next number with Mick Jagger appearing on a tower 23 metres above the set.

In *The Wall*, the symbolic wall structure (again of giant proportions) is designed to self destruct. The technology included polystyrene foam blocks, complex cages of light steel work and cables as well as dynamic lighting sequences. The suspended structure, the wire lace work, the implications of the spider's web now have an accumulated body of knowledge behind them. In combination with canvas or plastic structures, they were already being used by Le Corbusier in his *Temps Nouveau* pavilion of 1937. But the full potential of cable-hung tented structures has really been forwarded by the work of one man, Frei Otto, who already by the 1950s had made a series of small shelters and dance pavilions. By the time of the Munich Olympics in 1972, the combination of cables, nets and fabric could form a major, urban-scale structure. Otto's later work has looked increasingly towards the phenomena of nature and biology. This work, along with Buckminster Fuller's inspiration, has moved the twentieth century process of structure and invention from a series of mechanical feats (that were the inspiration of the nineteenth century) towards a polyvalent and extraordinarily active territory.

The next generation of new structures will almost nonchalantly incorporate overlaid techniques for heating, sound, atmosphere, light, moisture, simulated conditions; virtual reality as well as mixed real-and-virtual, all mastered by ever increasing feats of 'Look! No hands' with 'Look! Nothing you've ever seen before'.

CREATING THE SKIN

*House at Higashitamagawa, Itsuko
Hasegawa, 1987*

Skins and the Ground

In the last chapter, the skin was already being referred to as something with its own volition, but to give the word full power, it needs a special definition. The skin of the human body is essentially fused to the flesh whereas that of a building need not be. Even though they both have the function of facing the air, water or any other impacting condition, they both need to be cleaned and looked after. They are both the readable component of the body.

This relative fickleness in the relationship between skin and body had its origins, as we have already seen, in the development of expertise or 'craft'. The inevitability of the 'specialist' who goes beyond the simplest of processes of heaving around pieces of timber and stone begins to demonstrate the delight of those pieces. There are unending parallels between the human use of cosmetics and the cultural development of the facade. The painted lip has to deal with eating lunch; the sweetly fashioned doorway has to deal with the entry of a horse and cart. From this will emerge a complex language of fashioning that relates both to the celebration of events that occur on a facade along with the different pressures put upon them. If a doorway really did have to accommodate a horse and cart with any frequency, then it would soon be constructed with tough stonework (probably curved or 'buffed') to prevent battering by the cart.

The first question that has to be asked of any skin concerns 'hermeticness' which will probably involve tradition and culture as much as any more constructional factor. The cooler zones have a need for wind, rain and snow to be kept out and even more insidious conditions of dampness will have to be dealt with. In grey northern places, light is a precious commodity and sunshine, after a long winter, is to be celebrated. Thus begins a continual debate between the logic of solid protection against the weather and the craving for light and sun. Such a hermetic attitude is not needed beyond the Mediterranean where cool, dark corners are to be celebrated. There is little need for any seal to be achieved around openings, except maybe for security, and though mass still remains the most efficient means of insulation from both heat and cold, it can be cut into very simply. Hence the tradition of the detail-free stone blockhouse.

Before the twentieth century, this discussion would have revolved around the languages of decoration and formalism that surround the basic envelope. The discovery of iron and steel, the use of machines with which to cut wood, the progress towards manufacturing larger and larger, then tougher and tougher sheets of glass had just about been absorbed by a hungry industrialised society in the 1930s when further explosions took place with the use of aluminium alloys and plastics as well as new adhesives. The languages of decoration could become languages of intermixed devices that could choose to present themselves as representations of traditional cornices, awnings, doors or windows, but might well be something quite new technologically and even conceptually. Or, of course, they could delight in presenting themselves as something new. At a conceptual level, the very primacy of skin in relation to any other aspect of shelter should be enough, but we are dealing not only with the basics of survival, but a language that has to be interpreted for reassurance and recognition by the onlooker.

We can look outside architecture for parallels in the intellectual argument for or against 'honesty' in the representation of objects from which we need to exist. A vegetarian cutlet can represent itself as something in the shape of a piece of meat, as an abstract shape or a heroic attack on 'carnivorousness'. A car can be 'sporty', 'comfy' or 'rugged' and still have the same technical specification. We are all familiar with the sight of a concrete frame down the street, and that period of a few weeks in which we guess what the skin will look like. We all wait for the sight of an opening panel in the sheer glass wall or the promise that it need never open.

Layers and Membranes

Society now demands certain responses from the skin. At the extreme end, it may demand an impeccable degree of defence; every orifice gridded so that not even a child could enter, the entrances positioned so that surveillance is perfect and the main envelope of the building arrived at after a series of other barriers. The battle with the weather has been one of gradual, accumulated morsels of progress; full of compromise and optimism. There are occasional floods in Los

Angeles and the thin, boxy walls have to respond to forces that would be nonchalantly shrugged off by an old Helsinki villa. It is, quite simply, boring to have a very careful skin, with every window shuttered, protected, multi-glazed and every wall tailored for the occasional storm of hail. More interesting is to note the transference of skins from place to place. The assumption that the sea coast will encourage freedom and sunlight suggests large runs of glass doors and openings in odd places that will pick up magical views. The notion of the 'townhouse', even in cities that have no tradition of 'towniness', suggests an urbane and balanced facade, with order and even hierarchy. The corporate position suggests that the details of the skin should be sharp and elegant, and the scale of the elements larger rather than smaller. The ubiquitous skin and the 'front' and 'back' aspects must be dealt with, using cheaper materials where the public is less likely to notice. (A certain connoisseurship has grown up in which the keen observer finds out the 'true' form of the building by looking at it from the yard behind and functionalists can opine that the back is far superior to the front.) A more complex expressionistic issue concerns the amount of architecture that needs to be expressed. As you start to design the skin, it is helpful to have a clear attitude to this. You may feel that the whole thing should be uneventful and the window openings all the same. This will in its turn call considerable attention to the edges of those windows. What else is there to look at? Alternatively, there may be the desire to express every nuance of the internal sociology, with the box room celebrated by a very small aperture and fifteen sizes of opening between that and the greenhouse. The observer will be reading so much into this series of messages that he can be forgiven for standing outside and plotting progress from the bathroom to the washing machine as if contemplating a map. We are, once again, close to the issue of elemental expressionism that characterised Chapter Three.

Shadowing this issue is that of the architect's preoccupation with geometry. The twentieth-century envelope has reasserted the horizontal line. That the vertical line must survive is explained in the previous chapter, and that the openings are the articulation of all points of view is an underlying theme of this chapter; their

Eurostar Terminal, Nicholas Grimshaw, Waterloo Station, London, 1994

Tin-faced house, La Boca, Buenos Aires, late nineteenth century

Johnson Wax Headquarters, Frank Lloyd Wright, Racine, Wisconsin, 1936-49

attachment to chosen geometry. Very few buildings are courageous enough to really become formal skins with drifts and diagonals, folds and undulations. A characteristic of the developments of recent years is rather to be found in the search for seamlessness. The 'magic' of the silicone joint, the shining, almost jointless granite face, the only-slightly billowing strips of timber, all celebrate the intention of a skin to be a conceptually seamless envelope.

It is as if the assertion of one geometrical direction only increases the magic. For example, in Frank Lloyd Wright's headquarters for Johnson Wax at Racine, Wisconsin (1936-39) the 'banding' of the thin window strip is extreme and the more the building changes the direction and size of its curves in plan (which it does, extensively), the more evocative it seems as an envelope. Moreover, the window strips are made from horizontal glass tubes, dealing unashamedly with the issue of illumination and language, but looking quite unlike anything in the previous history of architecture. Then, with entirely different tastes and detail, Jacques Herzog and Pierre de Meuron make another horizontal shed, for the Ricola company at Laufen, Switzerland (1986-1991). The material is eternit cladding panels on a timber frame (and is symbolic of stacked timbers, characteristic of the sawmills in the area). Instead of Wright's banding, the Rationalist instincts of these architects is towards a cornice-derivative timber articulation of the top (albeit ironically fragile). When looking at Miralles' Alicante building in Chapter Twelve we shall also see evidence of a truly late-twentieth century nonchalance about the whole 'skin' thing, when pieces of cladding are hung out here and there as virtually free standing quotations of surface. The body stands out as it feels able to.

Such a point in the evolution of a tradition is evident in many other instances, if we have time to study the drawings or look hard for clues. Stonework, tiling or timber cladding can be hung onto galvanised steel hangers, with an air gap and various modes of insulation and weatherproofing to the main carcass, thus acknowledging that the skin can technically be peeled off – a mere veneer. Yet the development of the 'curtain wall' was, in its time, a major plank of the Modernist position. To finally enjoy the technological ability to separate the

Storage Building, Jaques Herzog and Pierre de Meuron, Lauten, 1986-87

West Hollywood reflected in the skin of Cesar Pelli's Pacific Design Centre, 1971

edges of the building from the carcass suggested that this could offer a certain sheerness to the outside surface. It could deal with pattern, components and geometry with a certain freedom. To see Norman Foster's Ipswich building set down amongst the Victorian and Edwardian jumble of downtown Ipswich was for me a particularly evocative sight since I lived in that town as an adolescent and had dreamed of an ultimately Modern world in the years between. To suddenly see its ability to be abstracted – scaleless, almost black, yet acting as a reflector of the remembered town, as if a ghost or a video image of the past – is not repeatable.

If the period of the heroic curtain wall is preoccupied with the issue of independence from all of the knotted intricacy and solid compounded nature of the inner building, there is now a second or third generation of technological skins that offer alternatives. In the first, a series of those same 'knots' are able to be threaded amongst the parts of the envelope. Heating, air conditioning, insulation, sun protection and fire prevention runs are the most obvious. There can be others, more particular to the needs of specialist buildings such as hospitals or storage sheds. It is partially (but not exclusively) a technical argument that will take some of these runs along with the visible 'grain' or predominant direction of joint of the skin. Some designers still feel more comfortable bunching these items at certain column or duct points, thereby, in a sense, extending the inside intricacy to the face of the building, effectively compromising the spatiality of the skin territory. The 'spandrel' condition (the part of a curtain wall below traditional window-sill level) is another repository of all manner of devices. It proves to be more than a fireproof panel and again, the 'skinness' is compromised.

We then arive at the third generation, which is analogous to the first, at least aesthetically. Here, the skin – the product of the new technologies that include 'smart' glass, electronics, fibre optics and time-controlled devices – may even be constructed entirely of glass, but have the ability to heat and protect, be fire-protected and climatically variable, without much in the way of threads and knots. The designer of clever envelopes can justifiably present a built element of creative ambiguity since a noticeable physical presence is not a necessity, although that may be difficult for the discussion of aesthetics.

Sir Norman Foster and Partners, office building (detail)

'Roof Roof House', Ken Yeang, Kuala Lumpur, 1983 (Yeang's own residence)

Having distanced ourselves from the carcass, we can argue that the freely-skinned building is, in fact, two buildings: the inner and the outer. Re-erecting our accumulated reasons for placing objects, setting up languages and evoking consistencies, we have to ask whether it is logical for the language of one to reflect the language of the other? Could a highly Rationalist carcass legitimately support a flippy-flappy expressionist skin? It can be done technically, presenting little operational illogicality, and it could be argued that this would absolutely demonstrate the sophistication of the built form. Alternatively, a sheer and ordered box could be filled with chambers of every mould, plan forms of exotic variety, looking like a map bounded only by the printed page. The rationale would read the same as before, a counterpoint ready to be played between the two buildings.

The orthodox position on all this might be to suggest a formal linkage between the geometry and aesthetic of the inner and outer buildings, with a clear difference of scale and interval between the one and the other. Yet such orthodoxy (with which we are only too familiar) often seems to have throttled the curtain wall. It is almost as if the totally 'lumpen' building has more power, more conviction and that the best curtain buildings are those with virtually no core condition. A developed sense of space (which will be discussed in Chapter Ten) needs to anticipate the way in which the magical qualities of the free envelope can be prepared for by the unravelling of the inner building.

Standing aside from these dilemmas is the position that can be taken by the building that deliberately loads the skin and makes it consciously substantial. The creation of a membrane of sufficient integrity and facility establishes much of the activity of environmental support: so that the inner building is effectively released from much of its servicing and is therefore somewhat 'balanced' with the membrane. Organically, it is a different proposition to the curtain wall and equally so from the 'expressive' facade of windows and special objects.

Buildings with *brises-soleil* or buildings with more than one layer of structure attached to the envelope are to be considered in this category, the ethos being that the more items of systematic and architectural significance set on the plane of the envelope, the better. If tempted – and there is certainly a temptation if one has a taste for wearing one's heart on one's sleeve – the result must surely be tempered by thinking through the quality of light and the quality of transparency or solidity that is created. Membranes can be wonderful, but they can also be obsessive if taken to a level of over-technologised fanaticism.

Facades

My shift of buzz-word is deliberate. There is not only something more archaic about the facade than skin, there is something more mannered in its overtones. Perhaps we can trace the history of the facade to the history of the street, in the same way that we might trace the history of cosmetics (or the face mask) to that of the formalised ceremony. In other words, this business of 'face' and 'facade' is all to do with pose and message-giving, philosophically concerned with quite separate (and more complex) issues from those of survival function or organic

Street scene in King George's Street, Tel Aviv

'Orderly' housing in Germany

Golden Pavilion, Kinkakuji, Kyoto, 1358-1408

Street scene in Shinjuku, Tokyo

Spiral Building, Fumihiko Maki,
Tokyo, 1984

Studio House, Notting Hill Gate, London,
c1880

Boatstore, Royal Naval Dockyard, GT Greene,
Sheerness, Kent, 1858-60

De Volharding Co-Operative Building,
JWS Buys, The Hague, 1924

Suburban house, Hove, Sussex

Hotel, Anton Rose, Copenhagen, 1912

Swimming Pool, Christoph Langhof, Sports Centre, Berlin, 1986

Spooky House, Ascots at Toowomba, Queensland

Arsenale, Venice, Bartolmeo Bon, 1416 62

House for a painter, Gustave Strauven, Brussels, 1903

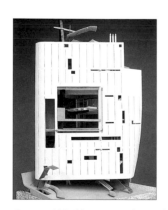

Commercial Building, Peter Wilson and Julia Bolles-Wilson, Tokyo, 1989 (project)

stability. Might one even suggest that the facade has more to do with architecture than building?

There is plenty of architecture that is driven by the facade. There is plenty of architecture, too, that establishes some main features of the facade that must be sustained for the first few moves within, such as the grandiose entrance leading to the equally grandiose central space or the diminutive wing with its suitably diminutive interior scale which leaves the rest of the facade but an abstract composition. In the comparative spread of illustrations, on pages 96-97, there is a range of pictorialisation but also a range of feedthrough from the facade to the inner workings of the building. Once again, the mainstream position on all this suggests a degree of feedthrough, until it becomes too difficult or too demanding of architectural sophistication, at which point the connection is visually relaxed.

Fiercer or firmer architecture takes a range of positions. First, that the facade is the architecture (therefore every major element that is measurable on the face of the building is reflected in the plan and every orifice in the facade is directly contributing to the light quality and thus the spatial quality of the interior. Secondly, that the facade is a total composition in its own right; it must have a completeness (which does not of course necessitate axiality though it may be the product of it). This completeness may or may not feed into the interior. Thirdly, that the facade is a free thing; asserting its own architectural characteristics. Fourthly, that the facade is a screen through which the real architecture will be perceived. This last aspect is especially suited to the glass skins already discussed, though screens may be defined by structural members in a consciously layered presentation, in a somewhat similar manner to a traditional theatrical tableau.

A virtuoso trick that cannot be considered 'standard' is to set up certain objects or features of a facade that are 'driven' into the interior: that is, given a very strong role in the plan leaving the rest to be of little or no impact. To be really cute in this game it is considered too simplistic for these 'driven' conditions to spring from the traditionally major elements such as the main doorway. In parallel is the notion that a facade can have a few significant elements 'drawn forth' from it, not as truly self-sufficient parts, but as a three-dimensional attack

Art Nouveau bay window, Brussels, early twentieth century

House at Silver Lake, John Lautner, Los Angeles, 1963

Spiral Housing, Zvi Hecker, Ramat-Gan, Tel Aviv, 1981-89

outwards from the main facade plane. The most frequent example is the balcony. An element that is almost always subordinate to the main wall face, it nevertheless combines aspects of the casual marking of an orifice, or the explosion of the room outwards from interior to say hello to the outside world and to then retreat. Alternatively, the balcony can effectively become the most dramatic articulation of an otherwise modest composition.

Facade-driven designing is not often admitted but does play a major role. Many of us work at a design, thinking and visualising our way towards an image or a goal set by a series of composed parts. A useful exercise is to draw an immediate 'scribble' plan of the likely consequences of the frontal image before modification. It was perhaps part of the reaction away from the pictorialism of the Ecole des Beaux-Arts and the excesses of the nineteenth century that suggested to Modernist teachers that an insistence on letting the plan drive the composition was to be made. I was taught this way: assembling the building as a series of layouts, testing them as a series of sections, manipulating those sections with light openings and overhangs and changes of level in order progressively to develop a series of consequent spaces. I was encouraged to develop the same project in parallel as a series of models that would test these plans and sections over and over again in different modifications and then, only then, see what the elevation might be. As one became more confident, one would 'tweak' a look at some trial elevations ahead of the approved sequence. It was assumed that the consequent elevation would be inevitable and not subject to imposed style. I would still advocate this as a most creative procedure and far more investigatory than trying to fill up behind a facade, but I would also advocate the open use of the 'tweaked look' if possible as a series of 'dips' into the future of the project.

One of the hardest, but most intriguing architectural pursuits, is to set up a nonchalant or a deliberately deceptive facade. Highly decorative architecture can do this the most easily, but it should be tried together with a stringently narrow set of *partis*. The exercise may choose to set up a few decoy elements, or it may choose to use the facade as 'slipped' architecture rather like a piece of lingering harmonic in music.

Orifices

The history of doorways is not only a history of power and protection, it is also a history of drama as we discovered in Chapter Four. The celebration of major doorways can be spread out from the actual zone of operation around a large territory, as if a whole patch of the building is intensifying towards the event of its explosion. In Modern architecture the entrance condition can be a part of a simple series of planes and recesses, somewhat in the manner of a *bas-relief*. In this case, the envelope is to be considered as total composition made up of three-dimensional parts – none of which necessarily demand deep space. Indeed, in this context, the door itself may be the deepest space.

As the materiality of the facade becomes more abstract, the use of 'cuts' into it can result in a mannerism of intriguing potential. Previous architectural mannerisms have tended to invest doors and windows with paraphernalia that accost the viewer and concentrate too much on the rim of the orifice, whereas the simple Modernist 'slit' (or its Mediterranean antecedent) leads straight towards the space beyond. The forward celebration (or protection) of the door is similarly a question of attention. Too much attention (pediments, steps or rich decoration) tends to stop the building in its tracks. It may in fact become a virtual 'building that stands before the building'. The Modernist vocabulary is again the more generous towards the setting up of a variety of spatial significances.

The spatial conditions that are possible with the articulation of windows seem at first to follow the same rules as those for doors, but there are other compositional responsibilities. Some are to do with repetition, some with range. The doorway is still a functional element of deep significance, the point of initiation, and most often identifiable with the human dimension. The opening of a window has nothing like the same symbolic or functional significance as the opening of a door. There is a certain innocence to the placing of a mere window to alleviate the internal condition. There is no need for it to make any particular statement; all the more delicious it is when a statement is made. The temptation is to define the position of all the windows upon a completely external composition. Some architects care very little that this results in internally meaningless positions and seem to prefer a certain abstractness or even the resulting abdication of 'responsibility'. The completely opposite pursuit takes a decided stance in relation to every window position. The question of profile and location really becomes interesting when you allow the device to push forwards. Sun-seeking and view-seeking cultures have pushed certain windows outwards. The English suburbs are filled with bay windows, but elegant examples having existed since Jacobean times. We now have another set of definitions that become a fundamental ambiguity.

The facade can be punctured by windows that are latent and repeatable marks. They can be recessed to emphasise the 'bodily' quality and therefore the dominance of the containing wall. They can sit with innocence in the middle plane of the wall. They can be on the surface, and in certain cases, sit deliberately amongst solid-backed glass panels (so that the rhetoric of the window itself is

Cemetery at Igualada, Enric Miralles and
Carme Pinos, 1985

Shonandai Cultural Centre, Itsuko
Hasegawa, 1988 (detail)

Air Rights development, Eric Owen
Moss, Culver City, California, 1995

subdued, or even ambiguously present). They can protrude as 'bubbles' on the surface of the facade. Once again, a clear understanding of these messages can add meaning and power to the composition of a building.

At the most complex level of creating facades, there is the possibility of making folds or vents, of contriving planes or undulations, of scattering decoys or cuts, of percolating the outer skin by an ever-threatening but ultimately conducive series of interferences of surface, without which that surface would be bland. The mysteries of a skin or a facade are most evocative when the issue of geometricised interference is turned into the equivalent of a piece of symphonic scoring – full of statement, theme, counterpoint, rise and diminuendo.

Skins and the Ground

We can regard a building as an 'artificial' object. Thus we can regard its skin as the ultimately artificial condition. Despite the objectives of 'organic' or 'contextual' or sensitive 'material-wise' envelopes, they cannot really be grown. The material eventually heads for the ground and almost inevitably has to be marked with a rim. There are, of course, a few underground buildings but even these seem to generate outcrops which themselves have all the characteristics of larger built objects. One anticipatory device (borrowed from the language of castles) is to sit the building on a mound. The mound can be of grass, it can be abstracted from the mannerisms of the main envelope or it can be fashioned from the same materials as the building itself. In other words, what is created is a 'skirt' condition.

Classical architecture was, of course, adept with 'edges'. The base might comprise that big, marked banding, or it might be the whole dramatic underscoring of the rusticated base whereby the heavy chunks bed down the building. Twentieth-century skins prefer to 'glide' onto the ground surface. On the other hand we encourage a physiognomy of scattered, tumbling elements and if they are intentionally 'organic', as are many of Frank Lloyd Wright's works, we can delay the moment at which we have to choose just what is the edge and what is the ground proper.

Do we want our building to grow out of the ground? Do we want the implication of incursion? Do we think that the envelope is really a figure? Is it the tradition and manner of the city that virtually demands a clear figure? Is the horizontal base line something in the manner of a platonic ideal? Is it necessary for the facade to be free, total and independently articulate?

Once again, the choice for the designer of a facade, skin or envelope is concerned with clarity of intention, even to the extent of discriminating between those three definitions. Remember too that in this phase of the analysis, apparent simplicity can be teased by wonderful incidentals, strange decoys, intriguing crevices, strange byways, ambiguities of surface and the possibility of even masking the mask itself.

Towers, Raimund Abraham, 1982, (project)

Tower retained from city wall, Frankfurt

Entertainments Tower, Peter Cook, Montreal, 1963

Hongkong and Shanghai Bank, Norman Foster, Hong Kong, 1985

Cathedral at Santiago de Compostela, Spain, 1168-88

Hochzeitsturm or Wedding Tower, Mathildenhöhe, JM Olbrich, Darmstadt, 1907

KEY CONDITIONS

Towers

There is a whole architecture contained in a tower. It is a total operation which can span from seriousness to frivolity or intense activity to blandness – all within one composition. Moreover, it will always tend to be read as a single, identifiable element despite the mixture of its contained components.

The tower separates or distinguishes itself from the surrounding context (whether building or landscape) by its essential assertiveness as a form. This is so, even if it is made from the same materials as buildings surrounding it or even if it is joined to them and has identical details. As an enduring symbol of 'otherness', the tower has a history of authority, communing into the skies directly to God, or having the advantage of long views and detachment during battle. If it has moved on from its historic significance to the Church and the Military, it has retained a status in the mind of the most innocent of bystanders that is still to do with this essential authority. In the twentieth century it has gained an additional role, both as total building or as key element.

The argument for high-rise development of a downtown area or a key commercial location (such as a 'business park' or the intersection of Wiltshire and Westwood Boulevards in Los Angeles) is not simply to do with land values; it is to do with prestige and identity. If we consider the Centre Point tower in London we know that it has sometimes been reviled and sometimes loved, and it is certainly not an exceptionally high tower. Yet, it has sufficient stylisation, sits exactly on a key crossroads and is isolated from other high structures so it has become a landmark; the exact successor of the old parish church of St Giles that sits somewhere at its feet. Even in Manhattan, it is possible to identify place and 'flag' from a distance, but in this context, the particularity of the tower (since there are so many) begins to be an issue; all the more so since the basis of the commercial high-rise is to do with the ratio of space that can be given to business in relation to the amount of space given to access and servicing. This 'gross to net' ratio has become a fine art in the late twentieth century and the envelope – which is what we actually see – is a matter of secondary choice as highlighted in the last chapter.

The most intriguing of the world's favourite icons is the Chrysler Building. Even the most hardened Rationalist is unable to succumb to its strange combination of exaggeration and elegance. It is as if the architect William van Alen had really succeeded in combining the scale of the styled top and Art Deco entrails whilst gauging these to the proportion of the building bulk and the degree of impact seen across and down town. In the same way that Centre Point dominates London's Oxford Street, the Chrysler dominates New York's Lexington Avenue, albeit more deliciously. But the issue here is more subtle and more political. The tower building has the scale of its height so that a piece of architectural substance – a protrusion, wing, the appropriate expression of windows, strips of windows, set-backs of roofs, balconies or entrances – has to be identifiable at a scale that is compatible with the vertical presence (maybe hundreds of metres high). But it also has to make sense to the nearby viewer who may also be the user. The adoption of high style in the case of the Chrysler Building suited a high-style commodity: the proud American Car. It also suited a high-style location between midtown and the upper East Side. More significantly though, there was just sufficient latitude in the demands placed upon the designers, to flex the rules of 'gross-to-net' ratios to produce a composition of parts, rather than an optimal envelope. Pre 1950s high-rise buildings tended to use a compositional mixture of formulae, by which the stacking up of vertical space was combined with the stepping outwards of the building, all of which was calculated to fit within prescribed rules of daylight angles. Two developments then started to move against this. The first was a spiritual and stylistic detachment from 'modelling' – the carry-over from the Pure Modernism of the complete box – and the eager recognition by developers' architects that this would lead to more simple, and therefore more standardised parts whereby the floors and components could be the same and the skin cheaper. The rules were partly changed and partly manipulated and the commercial tower (often a slab) was born.

In a sense, the subsequent development of the office or housing slab has reduced the distinction of high buildings in one's mind. There is no dividing line between a rather high long block and a rather low high-rise slab. It is almost as

The Lloyds Building, Richard Rogers Partnership, London, 1986

Typical industrial suburb, Tokyo

Typical downtown night-time scene, Tokyo

if the street-side system of building had become able to place itself upon itself, made possible by the invention of the lift. There can be a vertical heroism, however, and its definition involves a fundamental issue. When is a tower not a tower? When does a vertical building gain a detached personality? The answer is either to do with proportion or, occasionally, to do with the celebratory top (discussed later). The issue of proportion is both mythical but also primeval. How does primitive man recognise a mountain or a club held in the other man's hand, or a cutting instrument or a rock behind which to hide? Not necessarily by material or surface only, but by association of shape with size involving the proportion of such characteristics as 'edge'. The complexity of architecture sometimes hides the link between form, association and choice. Typologies become recognised by the untrained but experienced. So towers are immediately recognised as enjoying a special power, and the rents of apartments within might be just a little higher than in lesser buildings.

As a designer, one may wish to celebrate a particular event or need within the building to act as a 'badge' for the rest. The mannerisms enjoyed during the period 1880 to 1920 seemed to accommodate this particularly well. The corner of a street could be marked by a turret and not only did the inhabitant of the turret enjoy a certain distinction (and probably an octagonal or circular room) but the building distinguished itself among the hierarchy of the street.

For the organic, stylistic and economic reasons already mentioned, this mannerism has long been abandoned. In its place, the most likely outcrop at high level is the tank room and the lift motor room. They are not always combined and their random occurrence starts to give the roofscape a devil-may-care appearance which was particularly bad in the 1950s and 1960s. Recently, they seem to have been revived in a curiously successful way by the Asian enthusiasm for advertising. The Tokyo skyline — often criticised as chaotic – is enlivened by a wide variety of bright patches of colour which bear trade names, symbols or even identifiable objects coming out of the top of the supporting buildings. They often cover the tank room, lift motor room or air-conditioning plant. They may not be solid constructions – indeed, the best ones are not – but in a very roundabout way in a late twentieth-century world, they have rediscovered the medieval sign language of two associated symbols and made them one. The Japanese superstructure-sign is both tower and flag.

The inventive brilliance of the Chrysler Building top – always better than that of the Empire State Building – is only ever matched by the essentially slab-like McGraw Hill top, which appropriately sits over a slab-like substructure. William Piriera's Trans-America Triangle Bank, though often dismissed as a 'toy' by serious architects, remains endearingly successful in identifying downtown San Francisco, Ernesto Rogers' Torre Velasqua in Milan of 1957 succeeds as an icon of the city, despite virtually breaking the key rule of the inhabited tower. Here, the structure becomes more of a 'lump' at the top than the bottom, although there is a certain precedent in the traditional Italian *campaniles*, which were not inhabited.

At this point, albeit elliptically, the question of the tower as a complete typology is raised. In the hands of a spirited and discriminating designer, the idea of 'tower' and 'outcrop' can be held in the same frame of reference. They can both inhabit the same built mass. If one is prepared to accept thrust in the form of a wing of a building moving out from the main mass so that it has partly its own identity and, partly, the shared identity of the whole building, then all we have to do is to put the same proposition on its side. The Oslo City Hall by Arnstein Garneburg and Manis Paullson (which, incidentally, is the refinement over some thirty years of a competition-winning scheme), sets up two similar towers and binds them into an insistent total mass of building that still dwarfs most of the city. Compositionally, the tower is waiting to be brought in from its present state of torture, which is either to be remembered as a *campanile* or to be emasculated by its distant relationship to the high rise. Tight form, wrapped around an access core, has tremendous power as an organic type. It can be used together with horizontal extrusion in an architecture that escapes 'boxiness' without recourse to gratuitous pimples of form.

Another twentieth-century pursuit has led to tower formation that has never quite reached full fruition and is worth developing in the twenty-first century. Related once again to the invention and development of the lift, this type of formation associates other forms of 'threaded' support. The seminal example is Louis Kahn's Richards Medical Center, at the University of Pennsylvania in Philadelphia (1958-60). The simple idea of an uncluttered space being 'served' by the 'servant' towers needs no further elaboration in order to make a clear and elegant building. Though infinitely more intriguing, the Richard Rogers' Lloyds Building in London is based upon the same formula.

Certain castles provide a precedent, but they had only to deal with access and view plus a modicum of structural support if you consider a turret to be an elaborate form of buttress. The notion of carrying almost everything up in a minimum number of primary legs has wonderful planning potential. It comes close to megastructural thinking, but in this case it also provides a recognisable and essentially hierarchical base for the subsequent design, as if to say: 'First, the towers. Second, the floors. Third the rooms. Fourth, the windows'.

McGraw-Hill Building, Raymond Hood, New York, 1931

Peachtree Center, John Portman, Atlanta, 1976

House, Eric Owen Moss, Brentwood, Los Angeles, 1991

The idea of the tower as a 'stack' is another extension of language developed partly from the industrial, military and aerospace direction where a variety of pieces of apparatus are needed to be stacked and a framework of structure will provide a support for them all, but does not need to be filled up, nor necessarily 'skinned'. We are only just entering a world of commercial and organisational mix that can encourage the stacking, for example, of a hotel above housing above shopping above a school. Such a functional mix will certainly suggest a shift of architectural mannerisms and, once again, the reference to the total 'tower' may be of as much symbolic as structural use.

It is ironic that we are now in a situation where the tower may be a condition, whereas only some seventy years ago, there was the need to exaggerate the difference between its parts. The full cycle has thus been reached in terms of identity. For the designer, the real choice lies in deciding whether the tower is to be a container or a 'rack' – a raised total body.

Tops and Roofs
Already we have noted the significance of marking the top of a tower and the significance of profile when it comes to identity. We have also tracked the significance of the top surface in terms of structure and it certainly cannot always be assumed that the top of a building is a mere 'hat' with no structural significance, or that the outcrop – or any other statement made at the top – establishes the significance of the building's presence, its discipline, its rhythm.

In towns and cities, the roof makes a significant iconographic contribution to the whole. This is foolishly ignored by many architects of the twentieth century and by commercial pressures that assume that the passing car and the passing pedestrian have a primary role to play in the viewing of architecture. Yet there is the distanced, contemplative look and the less focused, but significant role of it as a constituent part of the 'quilt' of a city. Pitched roofs have a number of architectural responsibilities; they can be bland, running from end to end of a rectangular space; tedious and unworthy of further comment; or roofs which drape over a number of protuberances or indentations. These have to choose which parts of the substructure they wish to play with and then may, in certain cases, start to droop even further down parts of the building. There may be buildings in which the roof can actually integrate with the body of the building. In the Eric Owen Moss house at Brentwood, Los Angeles, the reverse occurs. The wall material (suitably coated with silicone) sweeps its way over and down the other side. Herb Greene's 'Chicken Shack' house at Norman, Oklahoma, is a comparable case of totality, whereby there is no particular element that can be called a 'roof'. Both of these examples are special and exotic designs, but they both suggest that the unspoken reason for the antipathy of many architects towards the 'pitched' or 'hipped' roofs is because of the banality with which they are usually set on a line, presents a dumb, inclined face towards the world.

The flat roof is inexorably bound up in the early twentieth-century battle for 'Modernism'. It may have to do with the attraction of the clarity of the white box

Kirin Plaza, Shin Takamatsu, Osaka, 1985-87

Roofscape cinema, Atsushi Kitagawara, Shibuya, Tokyo, 1983

Stockholm University Library, Ralph Erskine, 1986

Roofscape looking towards showroom building, Masaharu Takasaki, Tokyo (now demolished)

Lawyers' offices, Co-op Himmelb(l)au, Vienna, 1988

Cinema, Atsushi Kitagawara, Shibuya, Tokyo, 1983

Syntax Building, Shin Takamatsu, Kyoto, 1989

Townhouse, Schweinfurt, Bavaria

Industrial Installation, Warrington, Lancashire

Spiral Housing, Zvi Hecker, Ramat-Gan, Tel Aviv, 1981-89

Roofscape of Regency squares, Brighton

(along with its detail-less openings already discussed) that exists on the more exotic side of the Mediterranean Sea. Clarity is certainly a central issue. The flat roof can arguably be considered as the absence of roof. The architectural statement is then left to walls and their openings. If these openings are then behaviour or function-led, we have a direct message, without interference from the irrelevant 'hat'. Moreover, the profile of the building – the all-important diagram – could then be read by the observer below. Even better if the observer happened to be above, since, once again, only the diagram edge would be readable.

The flat roof suits the expression of identifiable 'lumps' or of a building. A pitched roof is always being gathered towards the apex, thus becoming a form of decoy away from the statement of the plan-edge. Other architects would argue that the diagram is of little interest and that the pitched roof is more humane, more weather-worthy, more implicitly protective and possesses more charm. Such a battle reminds us that behind the preference for manner or style, there often lurks a far more fundamental issue. One of motive. One of creative priorities. Is functionality more important than friendliness? Is the expression of primary conditions more important than romantic profile?

Having already noticed the Japanese city and its tops, we can begin to look at other aspects of current life and current technologies and ask whether we have fully exploited the possibilities of tops and roofs. In addition to water tanks, lifts and air-conditioning plant, there are now solar collectors. We have almost forgotten, too, the various frames, sub-houses and other devices that were beloved of some pioneer architects of the 1920s and 1930s, who believed in the potential of sleeping in the open air or at least of using the roof as a garden. Is it pollution or temerity that has interfered? In 1928 in West Hollywood, Rudof Schindler created a double house which was erected with minimal elements of wall, awning and screen so that he and the other occupants could sleep in the open air. From this we could, without the same enthusiasm, conjecture that a building has a certain regular roof datum, but has any number of superstructures outcropping upon it for special or occasional use. The 'penthouse' is a tame example. In a way, the contemporary enthusiasm for 'opening-up' lofts and incorporating them into the active body of the house, is analogous, but lacks any architectural verve.

A certain revival of the rolled-over or 'barrel' roof is an intriguing phenomenon. Allied to it is the shallow curved roof which often seems to be loosely 'laid' over the substructure; quite definitely a 'hat'. These forms suggest that the abstractness of the flat roof is not easily compatible with buildings that are intended to state the presence of an event, or that represent individualism in some way. The barrel roof emphasises geometry and virtually demands a total, rectangular shape down which it can drop. The shallow, detached curve suggests a deliberate avoidance of ponderousness or 'weight', as if a separate pavilion has landed. Le Corbusier's outcropping forms that sit aloft the first Unité d'Habitation at Marseilles (1947-52) make a statement of pavilions in a landscape; at once the landscape of the large roof itself and the landscape of the surrounding hills. Between 1982 and 1984, Frank Gehry's Work Residence remodels a block – where once again there is a total building placed above a regular slab – so that it looks as if it has just landed. The question of whether a top is of the building below, or can, like a canopy or a balcony, be considered as an appendage, is now open to creative debate. Moreover, the potential for many key parts of a building to be architecturally autonomous is recognised by technical demand and technological responses. Parts of a building can be separated screens, moving parts, rolled in or out, hung and collapsed, or nonchalantly inserted into a 'cage'. In 1992, Christine Hawley and I created a glass roof to a canteen in Frankfurt that opens and shuts in one piece and is treated as a working part rather than as a finite element.

With the cycles of fashion and the parallel cycles of psychological need that occur in architecture, the roof has a key role to play in the statement of 'mood'. In periods of self-confidence they may even disappear; in periods of caution, they cover and reassure; in periods of experiment they sprout extraordinary geometries and outcrops; in the 1950s there were wavy roofs; in the 1980s, shifty roofs. Thus seriousness and playfulness are linked together within this most critical protector from sun, rain, snow and wind. What irony!

The *piano nobile*

I have no particular intention to load the description of the Key Conditions towards a reinforcement or reintroduction of the language of Classical architecture. However, the present category serves a very special purpose: to identify a territory and to look at the hierarchical way in which buildings offer their facilities as well as their space. In other words, I do not believe that we design with a completely 'even' level of adrenaline. The highly rational, the highly mathematical and the highly functionalist might claim to be 'even' in their distribution of space but may still be able to absorb the instinct of privileged space and privileged location. For them the task is to weave it into an apparently equivalent language. Out-and-out expressionists have a much easier time. They can wallow in hierarchy as fulsomely as they like – the grand salon, the idiosyncratic shape, the stage for a major architectural experience set by detachment, elevation, cute lighting,

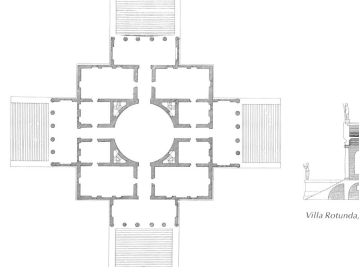

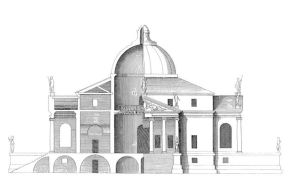

Villa Rotunda, Andrea Palladio

111

flights of stairs. Whatever lies within the vocabulary of the designer and the tolerance or pure enjoyment of the user is valid.

The origins of the *piano nobile* – the elevated grand floor – are various. It can be raised above damp or animal-ridden ground, raised in order to have a view, for privacy, or for defensive purposes. All of these reinforce each other. If the *piano nobile* is used for complex or public functions, it is readily appreciated that these are usefully supported by a 'sandwich' of ancillary floors that can send the necessary supporting people and activities up or down, thus making the key functions on the *piano* work smoothly. The obvious extension of all this is readable in the different heights that are given to the ceilings of the three floors. The height of the *piano* itself can become twice that of the floor below and remain perhaps one and a half times higher than the floor above. Inevitably the salons, the large windows, the auditoria and similar items must be on this level. As soon as such a formula is available, it can be stretched and reinterpreted. The typical Georgian squares of London established a 'basement' level below the 'ground' level, setting the *piano nobile* at the third constructed level – though it is only the second visible level. In a sense, the town house is narrow enough to need two main levels with subtle loading of values between the two.

The democratisation of architecture that is a characteristic of Modernism demanded a return of activity to the ground. Let it be there for all to see, for all to participate in, at least nominally. But the old habits persisted, for the 'sandwich' is such a useful idea. There is an inviolate logic behind making the key spaces higher, both for proportional reasons and those of air and noise. There is the basic need for ancillary activities. These cannot be placed alongside the main spaces except on a sprawling site. Thus an analysis of most twentieth-century buildings will reveal the continued use of a 'lower' floor, except that it is now pushed firmly out of sight and totally below the ground that must encourage the percolation of the public spaces.

As designers we should take note of all the implications that lie around our first sectional move. When we load a piece of space with significance, we are usually aware of its lateral ricochet effects but are too lazy to make the same analysis vertically. There are useful possibilities to break down the tyranny of both basement claustrophobia and the old grand detachment of the raised salon, should we wish. We can vary the section with half, third or quarter levels, weaving the opportunity of 'exposed' or 'revealed' space inwards and outwards. We can create an internal balcony or 'pit' that has the same effect, or return to raising the main floor with as much or as little accentuation of its architecture as we wish.

A fundamental issue that runs around this discussion is that of the building and the ground *per se*. Like mother and child they are bound together by a primeval relationship. The innate need of the building to relate to the ground and yet distinguish itself from the ground lies behind every piece of architecture. The delight of the horizontality or verticality of the stated object and its shape, of compositional resolution and all the subsequent gambits that sustain these delights, need the ground as reference. Even the building that 'floats' on pilotis is making a conscious gesture towards it. We have to consider this alongside the dynamics of the building itself, as an abstract, as a condition that coerces human action and responds to that action as it knows best: imagined, concocted, concentrated upon. The more intense the design, the more likely a powerful concentration of forces around a certain zone. So we have two powerful forces acting together, both aware or unaware of each other; the one primeval, the other cerebral. In place of the *piano nobile* we can consider a series of explosions or resolutions. Whatever they are, they are likely to provide a key to the subsequent playing out of the design.

It becomes impossible to discuss any resolution of this set of forces without discussing view, surface, apertures and, of course, context. The Classical *piano nobile* was, irritatingly, a useful tactic or semi-abstraction that provided a likely device for most resolutions of the issue. We should like to think that we now have more subtle and less undemocratic devices available, but these are likely to make much more stringent demands upon our resources of language and pattern.

At the urban scale, there are clues to a totally revised way of thinking about the issue, that can apply to city buildings. For the reality of the late twentieth-century city is one of dispersed or layered ground. The visible ground is a top surface above subways, underpasses, cables, drains, basements, multi-level parking and, in Japanese and Canadian cities, an underground 'city' of shops and even canals. A few buildings tap into all of this with panache. If we add the potential of 'dropping' sections along with ramps or other diagonals (thus threading the building into this three-dimensional condition), we have a 'three-dimensional city' previously only dreamed of by those who advocated the 'deck cities'. The ground inhabited by architecture at last!

Bases – and What Lies Beneath

Both the argument and the text are folded together. If the *piano nobile* was accredited with visible power and organic grandeur, then the base of the building was treated in a highly ambiguous way. Once more it became a cultural issue which was accelerated by the development of motor transport. Delivery of goods had been kept as a discrete activity, usually dealt with at the back of the building. However, the social and psychological attachment to the car changed all this. The business of arrival and of extending the ideals and attributes of the salon to the car itself began to place a much higher value upon the ground floor. The base became the level of interface with mobility and emancipation. In public and domestic buildings the car must be taken into the bosom of the architecture; sucked into the basement, or housed in its own pavilion. Perhaps this has been the true preserver of early twentieth-century ground worship.

Nonetheless, we have a curious relationship towards the tradition of the street. In many instances – shopping, for instance, an institutional activity as well as housing – there have been sophisticated series of detachments, replacements and decoys created to avoid danger and discomfort. Whether at the level of pedestrian zoning or simply setting a series of buildings above an underworld of parking, it is now unlikely that all buildings could return to a direct relation with the street as it was before the mid-twentieth century. In cities, we have devised raised podiums, plazas, decks, the sunken cities, we have carved into the bodies of our buildings. Many of them contain a third of their substance below ground. Once again, the designer must concentrate upon the section. Whether dexterity, ingenuity, formulaic manoeuvres or sheer vision, the forces can be seen to gather as they enter our building: we may have the mandate to prepare for this outside the shell (if the site permits) and we certainly have the mandate to organise the 'spread' within. The hierarchical separation of 'base' and *piano* suited a certain society. The clue to their replacement may therefore lie in designers' analysis and understanding of the behaviour and aspirations of the people within. Allied to an inventive section, the result might be even better.

Corners and Edges

The corner of a building is architecturally its strength or its weakness. As we can see from the 'corner' images, below and on page 115, the exercise of wit has been intense in history. Much of our attention has been given to the creation of organisation and form. Even in this chapter we have looked at key conditions that have a defined role or an almost independent history. Yet the corner is no such category. It is more of a handmaiden of the created form, or even its passive consequence. We should watch this passivity however, as the building is near to being bared or fractured, or brilliantly defined and bound. The moment of stretch and turn is the moment of truth.

We are considering integrity when we examine a corner. We are seeing clues as to the substance, grain and dexterity of the skin, but even with a rounded corner or one that is clothed in thin materials, we are seeing the play between integrity and continuity. They are not the same thing. Integrity may be created by a series of interdependent forces whereas continuity may be created by surface. The majority of buildings are designed by the making of line drawings. Position thereby emerges as the most dominant criterion; line establishes position. Substance is a subsequent issue and it may require a degree of contiguity when reaching

Eigen Haard Housing, Michel de Klerk, Amsterdam, 1913-19

Hoover Building, Wallis Gilbert, London, 1936

Paradise Restaurant, Gunnar Asplund, Stockholm Exhibition, 1930

the edge of its system. The question of architectural control and a clarity of purpose may well express itself in either emphasis of the corner or a truly deft relaxed approach. Twentieth-century architecture has enjoyed the gambit of cutting the corners by the insertion of windows that play with the idea of view and transparency as a paramount objective and at the same time point out the strength of the holding material (probably concrete). Late nineteenth-century architecture enjoyed celebrating the corner by adding a turret or a miniature turreted window at an appropriate moment. The increased use of glass has sometimes lost the art of emphasis and the corner strip of steel is one that just happens to be the last. In the beginnings of twentieth century 'technical' architecture, the delight in the building's skin, was emphasised by 'skimming' the corner by running round it on a curve. Jean Prouvé at Grenoble achieves this with originality and elegance.

The rounded corner is joyful, complete and surely makes reference to the power of the container; an extension of architecture's desire over the last one hundred and fifty years to carry on a dialogue with machine-made products. Smoothness has overtones of efficiency and totality. The building proclaims, 'I too am a commodity' and allies itself with appliances and cars in the process. Otherwise, corners can be aggressive, dynamic and thrusting. Zaha Hadid's heroic corner at the Vitra Fire Station near Basle of 1994 makes us aware of its totalness, strength, febrility and the memory of flight all at once. In a sense, this building (as so many of Hadid's works) seems to be generated by its corner. In this way, we establish a telling strategy, bringing forth a category of element that would normally be a mere by-product of the process of design, literally on the edge of the organism and reversing the forces. The edge gives the direction; within becomes the submissive mass.

As with the other key conditions, the process of definition, of assembling tasks, parts or edges becomes strategic rather than merely tactical or expressionistic. These are literally the conditions of dynamics without which a building remains a meaningless mass.

Workers' Club, Ilya Golsolov, Moscow, 1926

Schminke House, Hans Scharoun, Löbau, Saxony, 1933

School, Helmuth Richter, Vienna, 1995

SPACE

Heroic Space

Ultimately, the idea of space originates from the psychological pattern of human well-being. The small child develops through experiences; a combination of the familiar challenged by the unfamiliar. Imperceptibly he begins to tolerate sorties into the unfamiliar as long as they can be related to the familiar. Only later does he develop a taste for the 'dare' qualities of stepping into the unknown. Our comprehension of architectural space has developed along similar lines. The first buildings with which we are familiar are touchable, related to the home and to friendly adults, and only gradually do we develop an ability to extrapolate the characteristics of larger enclosures and add them to the accumulation of experience.

In Chapter Three the normal responses that relate to action and experience were discussed, but the emerging awareness of 'space' is altogether more mysterious. It may be argued that not all people experience it in the same way. Its psychological condition means that sensitivity to the limits or perceived limits of 'surround' will differ. Perhaps the jolly, self-possessed character will 'take places as they find them' or the nervously haunted or paranoiac will constantly be wondering *why* or *where* are things significant.

The comprehension of space is something to do with reference and measure, but it cannot be prescribed by establishing significant measurements. It is connected to the effects of light and shade upon objects and surfaces, yet it cannot be prescribed by any rules of light intensity or light/dark syncopation. It is affected by the perceived contrasts of condition: 'narrow', 'tight', 'continuous' or 'controlled' space to 'open' or 'released' space. However, there are no known rules of spatial choreography available so we cannot predict a good or bad spatial sequence.

Touchable things have their own sense of presence and already imply space as they range themselves in series, running away into the distance. The brain associates them and the experience of them, and an almost non-sensual but 'informational' experience is set up. Maybe it is the recognition of this that has prompted so many architects to emphasise the 'repeat' conditions by way of panels, pilasters, or any studied repetition of elements that read as an accumulation. Yet the experiential quality of space is not necessarily created by sheer size.

Swimming pool, Christoph Langhof, Berlin, 1986

Exeter Cathedral nave, mid-fourteenth century

By contrast, there is the magic of the untouchable; the awesomeness of a lofty nave disappearing into a dark, misty distance. The interior of The Peachtree Plaza at Atlanta by John Portman, though often criticised as 'kitschy' by serious architects, has managed to create this spatial drama by a combination of vertical repetition and seductive modelling. In such cases, the observer is captured within a theatrical and controlled interior.

Equally, the creation of significant space has been developed and studied as part of the Western tradition of architecture and urbanism. The use of the 'figure-ground' diagram, in which all built form is drawn in black and all open space is left white, was used particularly in the 1960s and 70s as the basis for critical discussion of the space proscribed by the built form. Certain sequences and ranges of enclosure or exposure were encouraged. Most desirable were sequences of corridor-street that could then emerge at a plaza that (ideally) produced eccentricities of subordinate space existing in corners or running off in unexpected directions, but always foreclosed in some way that was visually intriguing. Thus, the consideration of distance as well as the face of the enclosing wall are complementary to the business of revelation as one moves through the space. That this is somehow easier to analyse and observe in the dimension of a town, rather than within a single building, is worth discussing. Somehow one is freed from the issue of pressure upon the space in which one stands from the point of view of function or reciprocity with the surrounding buildings. The role of 'plaza' to 'townhouse' is easily understood and the plaza can be appreciated at a figurative and experiential level. Now let us put the same conditions (maybe scaled-down) into a building. The plaza is now a central space and the townhouse a part of the same building with its intricacies hidden within itself. There is now the issue of role so that the large space must relate to the rest. By implication, on its own scale, expression must be connected with the function of the rest. Experientially, if you forget the significance of the ceiling or roof, you could observe and analyse in the same way as before. You could plot a route through and consider the experience of the 'ground', or in this case, the larger and more accessible rooms. Sometimes it works. You can observe – and therefore you can design –

by way of the sequences of space and the delight of changes of pace and condition.

Heroic space need not be large; its creation is more an attitude of mind. The sudden creation of a long, uninterrupted, windowless wall in a building that is otherwise busy with incident, will suddenly celebrate the distance of a room, telling you of its length and of the sudden space contained within that place. The same statement can be made vertically, where a roof light (or 'lantern') throws light down a shaft and past a couple of balconies down to the ground. It is probably a cheap enough device, but suddenness creates both a coherence to all the parts around and a dimension that reminds us of the magic of contained space (created by the building) in the context of endless space (hinted at by the roof light).

Quite soon, we are involved in a wing of the compositional process where we contrive to place combinations of 'tight' space and 'long-dimensioned' space in juxtapositions where the contrast will not fail to be recognised. If the design can then incorporate some surprises and some modulations of the 'tight-open' formula, we begin to have a form of theatricalism or expressionism where space is being enjoyed for its own sake. The similarities with urban space and its enjoyment as theatre are surely apparent. With architecture, however, this cannot exist apart from all the layers of reasoning by which we define those same spaces. Logic, position, function, sequence, structure and the rest succeed in restraining the total indulgence in space for space's sake.

In designing a building in which the quality of space will be rich and significant, you can contrive many of the conditions by models and predictive sketches – of progressions of space, vignette-perspectives and computerised sequences. It must be remembered however, that referencing is critical; that all the parts of the building are reminders of reality or mystery, immediacy or distance. The drawing of sight-lines on sketch sections or on plans, the tracking of one's progress through a series of spaces and acknowledgement of the significance of a sudden opening, a change of direction, a diagonal view that reveals an unexpected piece of information about the building, all these things can be plotted. It is usually a long business, but creatively rich.

House, Eisaku Ushida and Kathryn Findlay, Tokyo, 1979 (courtyard)

National Library, Clorindo Testa, Buenos Aires, 1965-94

Choong House, Wood/Marsh, Eltham, Victoria, 1985

118

One of the most useful systems is to retain a mental, or even a formally collected 'bank' of examples; places visited that have memorable spatial qualities and a straight analysis of why (perhaps) they were great. Scale, relative scale, tight-open sequencing, light – and how it affected identification, detail, perception, theatricality – and all that was revealed as you moved through, are checked.

Humble Space

There have been various studies and theories in which the kitchen, that most potentially paranoiac of places, is designed as a tight machine and the position of all its parts is related exactly to the gyration of the body, the dexterity of the arms and hands, and the correctness of the cooking process! In some circumstances, there is a near-symbiosis with the body and its tentacles. At this point the 'space' as such is little more than an extension of the sense of touch, control and extended function. What is there to *see* at such close quarters? Yet there may still be a sense of space which comes directly from this intensity of identification.

The Austrian, Walter Pichler, has gone some stages further. An artist who has been fascinated by architectural issues and has been himself a source of inspiration to many architects, he has not needed to recognise functionality and has therefore created a series of small buildings. In the 'House for Wagons' of 1980, the 'Glass House' of 1981 and the 'Small Tower' of 1988 there is a tightness of enclosure around the presence of pieces of sculpture (as well as very precisely cut and located window openings). The building 'box' thus reverberates back and forth towards these contained pieces and the space between is of a total process, organically as well as experientially. The Styrofoam packing of an appliance would be the only point conceptually beyond this, although it lacks the play of space and light that makes the Pichler pieces significant.

What emerges here is the notion of evacuated space, of a starting point of total integration and the subsequent forcing apart or incision to create space. The role of the human being vis-à-vis his enclosure is the first moment of spatial recognition. Is it a direct extension of the mandatory quality of life? And should immediate space therefore follow a conscious programme of restriction or release?

Offices, Eric Owen Moss, Culver City, California, 1988-90

Abteiberg Museum, Hans Hollein, Mönchengladbach, 1972-82 (interior)

Installation Woman in Bronze and Lead, Walter Pichler, St Denis, Austria, 1991

Functional considerations, which usually become invoked before we ask such a question may thus be accused of acting as a moral-psychological decoy, which keeps everything sensible and straightforward.

Our attitude to domestic space as opposed to public space can however be openly observed. It has an accepted variation in language and an accepted variation in degrees of heroism. A house tends to be small and therefore has an immediate reference to the street, garden or courtyard. These conditions become a discussable part of the spatial system of the house; the placing of a wall that catches the sun, seen across a yard; the role of the window that frames the view before it; the placing of a window with a long view down a street towards a known landmark as if a 'camera' towards the outside world (in the case of the bay window it is forceful acknowledgement of the power of the outside space).

Returning inwards, the significance of the corridor is hardly matched by any other part of a small building. It is as if the implosion and the claustrophobia of the situation add a touch of magic to this metre-wide (and probably only six metre-long) space. The incursion of a light source or even the most simple of width variations add architectural quality. At close quarters, there is thus the dichotomous contrast between overloaded reference: the domestic objects, the 'touchables', the mass of detail upon which the eye might fall and the need to regard that which is related at a distance by accident or circumstance; the pleasant view or the idiosyncrasies of neighbouring buildings. Is the design process therefore charged? Is there a definitive difference between a public scale and a domestic scale? Does the design of the house have to be reactive rather than proactive when space is the issue? Contemporary pressures of economy have certainly closed some options where apartments, offices and hotels are concerned. Low ceilings and optimal room sizes start to deny any mandate for the *internal* condition to control space, so the 'camera' role seems convenient – the room with the view replaces the room that creates view.

The insertion of internal decoys, the placing of freestanding or re-entrant elements is worth pursuing. In the Museum of Decorative Arts in Frankfurt of 1984, Richard Meier inserts a series of cabinets and divisions of space that are,

Tsukuba Civic Centre, Arata Isozaki, 1979-82

Sir John Soane's Museum, Lincoln's Inn Field, London (1813). Exterior renovation by Julian Harrap Architects, completed 1995

like the rest of the building, set upon a series of geometrical shift-lines. Thus, the bland large rooms are given a spatial as well as a referential dimension which is greater than expected.

Space, Captured and Released

We can control the degree, direction and orientation of light sources. We can predict its behaviour in normal day-to-day or month-to-month conditions. We can also use filters, screens, obscured glass, clerestory lighting, deep-cut openings, wavy, straight or faceted walls, smooth or rough surfaces. Added-up, this is a rich vocabulary of devices that affect the way in which we see the condition of our enclosure. They hardly affect the position of anything, yet position is the key point of discussion of building. Clients, financiers, critics and even quite respectable architects are most concerned with placement, questions regarding where things go, how big they are, how they relate in sequence. Is it that light and space, the retinal issues, are superfluous, too tricky for comfort or too spiritual and therefore inherently bogus or expensive?

Interestingly, it is another of those ironics of recent history that find avoidance of conscious space-making as a tenet of both commercial designers and certain rational positivists who are otherwise quite sophisticated designers. Playing with the theatrics of circumstance is a spooky, romantic, self-conscious game. That truth is basic. A good sensible layout is a good building; life is too complex for additional heroics anyway. Yet even the avoidance of conscious spatial games does not leave a neutral situation. Travelling down the Rhine Gorge or Death Valley is not like travelling across Holland or Florida. A two-storey suburb is unlike Manhattan. Space is inescapable. Avoiding the evidence of the eye in order not to train the eye is sheer laziness. We have already noticed that spatial contrast can be appreciated by sequential experience. So now we have three modulating factors: position, light and moment-in-sequence. It is worth setting up a typical example: the long winding corridor at first reveals a noticeable increase in light level as you move along, but then a sudden diminution. This is accompanied by a change of geometry. Further along, there is a turn and a brightly lit end wall beckons. The source of its brightness is not apparent until you have reached the end. There was a clerestory window above and behind you!

In the Vitra Furniture Museum (see Chapter Twelve), Frank Gehry introduces you into a relatively calm space – after gathering you up through curling arms – but makes you progressively aware of extended space upwards by the exquisite placing of large apertures and the daring nature of his interference with his own generosity of light. This sense of 'squeeze-and-pull' does not actually complicate the plan and certainly enriches the experience. In the house/museum built by Sir John Soane at Lincoln's Inn Fields, London (1812-13), there are several pieces of contrivance involving clerestories and lanterns and the play of light within rather small spaces that exist as an equivalent to Bach's keyboard inventions: evidence of a complex and sophisticated designer's will to exact a concentrated 'presence' from each part of the building.

Convent Hall, Günther Domenig and Eilfred Huth, Graz, 1973

Team Disney Building, Arata Isozaki, Orlando, Florida, 1990

Museum of Anthropology, Arthur Erickson, University of British Columbia, Vancouver, 1971-77

Jewish School, Zvi Hecker, Berlin, 1995 (detail)

Clayton County Library, Scogin Elam and Bray, Atlanta, 1987

Doorway, Hector Guimard, Nancy, c1905

Living City Exhibition, Archigram Group: Chalk, Cook, Crompton, Greene, Herron and Webb, London, 1963

Kate Mantilini Restaurant, Morphosis, Los Angeles, 1986 (detail)

Charottenburg Town Hall staircase, Berlin, c1900

Stansted Airport, Norman Foster, 1991

Illusory Space

We now have more possibilities to create a kinetic experience of space than ever before. At the extreme end, is the potential to project into the maximum experience of 'space' by way of Virtual Reality apparatus. One step inwards is the combination of real spatial contrivance combined with electronics and lighting apparatus to create accentuated space. One further step inwards merely uses programmed lighting, and then we move further back through the contemporary range of materials that are able to screen and control and mix the intake of natural light.

In parallel are the ways in which we can play games with scale. Seamless joints, endless glass, controllable enclosure, roofs that open are not merely technological trickery. They give us a formal apparatus that can create a series of spatial conditions that are not necessarily limited to the material and structural hierarchies of the past. The effects of this upon our spatial ambitions can be traced back to the beginnings of the twentieth century. Larger and larger expanses of glass were not only breaking down the definition of 'enclosure' but creating a new condition (and identity) of space. It could now be marked and 'claimed' (by the technicality of enclosure), without being more than a partial conditioner of light or form. Yet at the same time it was usually more than a mere sliver of interference, a mist or a film. Glass has a reflective presence and some degree of mathematical interval of supporting or stiffening structure. This is readable; its regularity identifies in the brain and it sets up an intellectual if not an experiential definition of space. From here on, the issue becomes intriguing. If space is controllable and readable across several modes of recognition, there is the possibility of creating 'orchestrated' space with the recognitive and emotive moments jumping back and forth, from deep space via interfered space, from enclosure to near-enclosure, from dark, through muted light passing through a skin, to full open light.

If there seem to be overtones of perceived landscape here, it is not surprising. For centuries there have been designers of both landscape and buildings who recognise the tactic of setting up both points of reference: long focus and short focus objectives together with filters of trees so that the comprehended territory tantalises our abilities to settle down to a formal understanding of where everything is. Is spatial definition a game that exercises as well as stimulates our system of eye-to-brain logic? A part of this same tradition sets up the Neoclassical mansion itself as the starting point for a serial dialogue with the landscape beyond.

From the chamber we see the immediate space of the courtyard or terrace, and from this, the garden (where some of the discipline of the terrace is retained); beyond lies the calm and smooth territory of the 'park' and beyond that, some areas of countryside that are in the control of the owners of the house. The placing of trees, hedges, built objects and lakes is a series of semi-circumstantial contrivances that accost the eye and bounce an awareness of distance, definition or territory between them. We are aware of the scale of some of the nearby objects – the details of the room, the balustrades at the end of the terrace, the approximate size of an oak tree – but this recognitive support inevitably melts with distance. Yet we can appreciate it all as a continuous system. More recent social conditions eschew the control of so much space by a single person (and a single designer?) and as a result, we have to make our long-range references and melt our vistas as a reactive process in the hope that a single event does not always respond to the range of space.

Decoys of scale have always been used to diffuse the reality of space, by way of painted *trompe l'oeil* effects, by geometric devices and by straightforward screening. However, the greatest challenge to our inventiveness with illusion exists now, thrust between social responsibility on the one hand and extended technologies on the other.

Space versus Figure

We can pose the central question: if the figure of the building is logical, then is the search for space Romantic? Against this we can argue that a central issue of architecture is to create identity. Atmosphere is to do with identity. Awareness of 'place' is equally so. The experiential qualities of distance and closeness are certainly sensual, but the denial of sensation is ultimately a cold and inhuman imposition.

Seen as objects in space, our walls, protuberances and recesses are subject to the same argument. In the light of a certain detachment of today's urban architecture

Installation to industrial plan, Formalhaut, Frankfurt, 1986

Gardens of Schloss Würzburg, Bavaria, eighteenth century

Cemetery at Igualada, Enric Miralles and Carme Pinos, 1985 (interior)

125

from the complexities of reference that were encouraged in the nineteenth century, it is necessary to search for ways in which architecture can be less bland, dull, flat and characterless. Post-modernism failed because it tried to do this by way of 'flat' referencing, with few buildings that were developed spatially. Yet one of the problems of streetside architecture remains its 'full-frontal' presence. The figure of the facade tends to give you the whole story like a piece of graphics – all at once, so don't look for anything more. To involve the figure (and the plan) with a series of memorable spaces within, and to give some clues of this to the street, involves adopting a serial approach to the design. Moreover, it involves the designer in the testing of as many sections that can be taken through the key stages of this progression as possible.

We can read a building as a series of layers, or almost as a series of tableaux. We can even set up such layers and tableaux, given the right site. As with the planning of entrances, vestibules and major internal spaces, the issue of conscious progression is always with us. In this chapter one has stressed the experiential condition, but it is intrinsically bound up with the issues of process, habit, ritual, speed of movement, ability to stop and comprehend, and the ability of the chosen stylistic mannerisms to present a range of conditions.

So we look once again at the figure of the building, testing it for spatial opportunities, searching for the opportunity to progress through from condition to condition, each with its own spatial idiosyncrasy.

Urban Space

Earlier we drew analogies between the recognition of urban space and internalised space. There is, however, the more complex issue of the individual building; its identity, its mannerisms, its own need to be spatially articulated and its contribution to the total urban space in which it finds itself.

It is argued by certain architects that if the building is a consistent part of a whole urban series (a house in a designed group of houses for example) it has no need for its own spatial pretensions. Better that it is a mute box and that the distancing of one house to the next or the syncopation of the whole group

Fashion warehouse, Hiroshi Hara, Tokyo, 1986   *Typical 1930s London suburban shopping parade*

vis-à-vis the locality is the spatial statement. In close-knit conditions, this argument has a point; the space between is readable towards the interiors as in a series of interlocked courtyard houses, or in the case of a terraced grouping where the landfall, the terraces themselves and the oblique nature of the terracing give opportunities for memorable immediate space. Elsewhere, however, the denial of internal spatial discrimination has a certain dogmatic arrogance to it.

Certainly it is more difficult to programme the sequence of experiences from the ranging of internal hierarchies of room (and therefore space) along with the external hierarchies of flanking, distancing and vista-giving. These are the *urban* obligations to be set all along an imagined set of experiences: from bedroom to corridor; corridor to central space; central space through porch to yard; yard through forecourt to street (incorporating the recognition of adjoining buildings); emergence from the street; gradual distancing from the cosiness or familiarity of a local set of buildings and out into the *mêlée* of the city. It is a familiar enough experience, yet it has rarely been orchestrated consecutively. Surely this should be considered an essential exercise for urban design students.

Where the building is an insertion into an already existing urban space, it would seem easier. Yet our habit of mere acceptance of the mannerisms of the surrounding buildings is a denial of some of the greatest traditions of city-making. In the great merchant cities of the past – those that we venerate today – the architects of the Venetian Palazzi or the Antwerp traders' houses were able to serve the demands of the waterside, the bringing in of goods, the need for status and ceremony, as well as the recognition of the discipline of tight and expensive territory, while producing buildings full of a variety of memorable spaces.

The clue is given. To create space, the central ingredient is twofold; it is a combination not only of visual sensitivity but also of inventiveness. Fabric, profile, object, vista, reflection, they are all there to be observed, noted, woven, observed again, walked-through (mentally or physically) and then rewoven. What we have been talking about is as much to do with substance as the earlier, more obviously operational issues. But more than ever before, we need to observe. Acutely.

A PLACE TO LIVE

The House

For our purpose we can bypass the pre-constructive periods of caves, mud huts and human nests. Entering at the point where a foreknowledge of local materials, some tradition of construction and a range of choice begins to exist, we can concentrate on the issue of people – specific people – and space.

Immediately we face the fact that the range of choice, standard of craftsmanship, elasticity (or sheer size) of space and all the decorative symbols that go with them, are the prerogatives of the rich and powerful. Archaeologists soon find ways to tabulate remains of dwellings in a hierarchy: the 'Villa', the merchant's dwelling, the military dwelling, the hovel. More useful to us as designers is a sensibility towards the inhabitants' own sets of priorities. Having dealt with wind, rain, animals, intruders, sun or dampness, they still have the option to build small closets or leave large open rooms, to build shelves or platforms, to make verandas or not, to inhabit the area within a pitched roof or not. Immediately, social habits and aspirations are under scrutiny.

The house is a reflection of its inhabitants. In simple terms, therefore, all the designer has to do is get to know the client extremely well, put a series of spaces around that person, introduce a series of devices – even 'playthings' – around him/her and any anticipated companions, and then, stand back. If this seems too simplistic, too direct and somehow mechanistic, we are voicing not only a doubt, but a central question that exists as an *a priori* to all fields of architecture. Are we to intervene between natural and semi-educated desire? Are we to override habit and prejudice with our own habits and prejudices? Are we to reinterpret behaviour and attempt to reshape it? Are we to act as the agents of the future, of 'better living', whatever this may mean to us or them? Is our role that of physical interpreter of the obvious or is architecture a 'higher' and more essentially artificial process?

Most of us would have to admit to artificiality. The layers of evidence exist in the ten previous chapters: the discussion of the 'house' merely serves to concentrate the issue, since there is no longer a wodge of intervening conditions between you (the composer) and your client (the player).

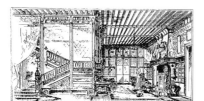

Yet a line of retreat from this vexed issue lies ready for both the architect and the user. For we are both products and victims of culture, which is an accumulation of codified recognitions of such matters as acceptable behaviour rather than instinctive behaviour. Symbolic luxury as distinct from real luxury. The trappings of comfort as distinct from real comfort. Almost certainly the users of the house will want to send out signals to their peer group and the architect may wish to do the same. These signals get crossed and confused, particularly in the case of more architecturally challenging work.

One route into this is the analysis of 'lifestyle'. The understanding of wishes as well as responses. Did a certain type of room really give all the opportunity that it might have, for the kids to romp around, the intellectual to concentrate, the invalid to bask in the sun, the cooking enthusiast to really indulge? Returning to history, we can trace a parallel issue: the degree to which the supporting society took the strain from the function of the house. In exposed conditions, this becomes a central concern. The trappers' hut up on the mountain, the lighthouse, the remote farmhouse have to provide some of the apparatus that cities or even villages can centralise. A simple equation can therefore be made between the degree of infrastructure or isolation and the consequent proportion of 'activity' space as against 'facility' space. Portable gas, mobile generators, land lines, the four-wheel drive vehicle have had their effect, but much of this equation survives. For the town-dweller, there is a more political analysis to be made. From the days of the cottages clustered around the castle for protection on to the paternalist and then Socialist support of the population in nineteenth and twentieth-century industrial towns, the house has only to provide for day-to-day fuel and appliances. In exchange for freedom of infrastructure, we have to locate the car. Until recently this seemed to demand a built structure, but this is increasingly retreating as the pressure for space is prompted by the increasing intensity of car ownership.

The simplest way in which to design a house is to break down the problem into a series of activities and form an 'enclosure' around each of them. By all means repeat the same enclosure if you can so that the same space is handling

House, Götz Stockmann and Gabrielle Seifert,
Frankenberg, Germany, 1994

Chicken Shack House, Herb Greene, Norman,
Oklahoma, c1960

Concrete House, Reykjavik, c1980

Sowden House, Lloyd Wright, Hollywood,
California, 1926

House, Heidolf Gurngross and Helmuth Richter,
Upper Austria, 1978

Bavinger House, Bruce Goff, Norman,
Oklahoma, 1950-55

House in Houston, c1955

House, Frank O Gehry, Brentwood, Los
Angeles, 1990

several activities. Very quickly in this process you start to reminisce about homes and houses you have known, people's habits you admire or dislike. Various pieces of anecdote and observation suggest that Le Corbusier's famous dictum, 'a house is a machine for living in', is rarely taken for granted. Moreover, even in low-cost one-room apartments, there is never a total lack of mandate; even the placing of the one main window onto a narrow street can either enhance the quality of 'lightness', 'privacy', 'total space', or emphasise the corner where you eat, you sleep or you read a book. Similarly, the placing of the entrance door can give long, short, diagonal or full-frontal views.

The main division in the history of the 'house' and the history of 'housing' revolves around the issue of identity. Most often this is seen in the form of separation. In history, the independent structure was either the product of isolation or power – the castle and the farmhouse – whereas in the walled city you almost certainly joined onto another structure. As with other building types, the street became a key generator, the entrance a key focus and the front facade a key representation of whatever you wished your house to proclaim. Even quite modest Georgian houses in London carried through the Classical dictum of lower storey, *piano nobile* and a 'minor' floor (or floors) above. Imperceptibly, however, the analysis of the rest of the same building begins to tell us plenty about the social and architectural splits. Is it totally logical to give an area for talking and eating a high, frontal space and give an area for washing and cooking a low, possibly dark and yard-facing space? Washing and cooking are messy, but probably have four times as much occupancy as the 'salon' if you conduct a person/time analysis. So the plan and hierarchy assume demonstrative overtones. Peer-group pressure suggested for centuries that the activities of washing and cooking were not only messy and smelly, but carried out by servants or members of the family taking on the part-time role of servants during much of the day. Only in the mid-twentieth century was this assumption really challenged and the place where you wash and cook was not only mechanised and miniaturised as far as possible, but the environmental quality of the place where you cook given high priority, with good views, prime space and some pride in its existence. Even now, this

Studio houses, Frank O Gehry, Venice, California

Carlton Terrace, Brighton, early nineteenth century

state of emancipation is denied by many societies and the plan form is a good barometer of social and gender attitudes in a culture. However, by simply looking at their own social experience, most architects can observe the aptness (or otherwise) of domestic space. The typical late-night 'architects' evening, with gossip, alcohol and books contains some rituals. The visibility of the books and selected icons (graphics, paintings, trinkets) are statements of an aesthetic or intellectual position. The detachment of the point from which you watch television from that at which you eat will of course be a product of the space available, but also of habits and gestural connections or barriers. Ideally, the design of the house is there to facilitate – or even accentuate – these things. The architect of the Victorian or Edwardian villa in England, or the *burgerhaus* in Germany would make sure that his client had a convincingly grand space commanding the best views as the major statement of the building. Quite modest and even inaccessible bedrooms might be the result of this major investment. The increasing cultural effects of travel encouraged the addition of conservatory or glazed terraces. If you or your friends travelled to the Orient, began to collects Chinese objects and read about mythology and the exotic, there would need to be a space in which North Europeans could breed exotic plants, smell their smells and indulge in reveries. Indeed, the study of appendages makes the most fascinating use of our social/architectural antennae. The present-day extensions made by bourgeois families to standard suburban houses reflect issues of health-activity, travel (once again) and the television-inspired significance of the barbecue.

The 'bay' window, discussed before, was a cheap and iconographically powerful symbol of 'space' and 'independence', and spoke much of the hidden frustration of the city-dweller constrained by the geometry of the street. The attention paid to the porch – both in European and American houses – speaks of aggrandisement, ceremony, social niceties with relatively little reference to waiting for the doorbell to be answered. The differences between American and European society are traceable here and elsewhere. The ethos of the 'American Way' is essentially that of a single society from which you may or may not emerge wealthier than your brother. The architectural consequences of this are allowed to be direct: wealth

House, Eisaku Ushida and Kathryn Findlay, Tokyo, 1990

Typical 1920s suburban housing in Brisbane

132

manifesting itself in the size of one's house, car, lawn, steak. However, in Europe, the hierarchies of family or job are presumed to be more static and the architectural tricks of making the most of a feature are allowable within a variety of rules of urban obligation. The distance by which an appendage (balcony porch, wing) may protrude from the main building line are also proscribed in the American house, and there is a certain 'image-totality' that is psychologically difficult for the tradition of European bourgeois behaviour. The statement that 'I've made it' can be catalogued: the conservatory is followed by the terrace, then the games room and then the pool. Again, in Europe the successful family is as likely to buy a second house in another place. Thus, the symbols of success are suppressed. Most frustrating for architects (from any aesthetic grouping) is the degree to which the client needs reassurance about the positioning and relationship of the rooms themselves and he tends to be conservative about privacy, openness or habits. Yet the same client may not mind radical or naughty things happening at the edges of the building. The design of a lifestyle is the most intriguing part of the whole process.

Running against all this is a fundamental paradox of order and survival. If a peasant family fought for their Duke, the Duke was obliged to house them. The implicit order of the army could be contrasted to the circumstance of the land: the placing of the cottage had not the same urgency as the battle lines. Nonetheless, the city wall would impose a certain discipline upon the form of the houses within it. Contemporary society has parallel structures. The supermarket shelves are enlivened by the representation of 'goodies' and commodities. A chicken can be compressed, folded and wrapped – to a degree – but must look like a chicken for you to want to buy it, but a baked bean need not have the same identity. The supermarket shelves give way to freezer cabinets because of display considerations, as well as those of temperature. In the same way, a highly opinionated, sophisticated, idiosyncratic city dweller is willing to be packed like a sardine in a subway train, only to demand space in the studio, office or bedroom. We have become conditioned to supplication – or is it subordination, albeit at a variable scale – in order to survive.

The designer of the house or the apartment must constantly recognise this paradox. We are no longer quite so locked into social and aspiration demonstration as we were in the closed societies that existed before the mid-twentieth century. Mobility and the internationalism of metropolitan life has seen to that. The architect however, has a new responsibility to reinvest the dwelling with meaning; a new kind of comfort; a new kind of release from the packaging of events. Soon, more than twenty per cent of these urbanised home-comers will have spent several hours of the day in front of a small digitised screen. If not travelling in the 'sardine' condition they will have been trapped for some time inside a vehicle that is con-stricted, predictable and restrained by slow-moving traffic. And then . . . Home!

Now to reassert the paradox. Much architecture is created (unwittingly) in the name of order, logic, simplicity, measure or process. We are living inside a segment of disciplined support that is reminiscent of the serried ranks of troops or the stacking of the supermarket shelves. The ways in which to carve out freedom, calmness, a backdrop for individuality, within all this is the central challenge to the designer.

Let us assume that there is a large plot for a house. The enclosure itself can be treated loosely; the only restriction is the edge of the garden. The family life has been investigated, the range of habits predicted. The next step is to decide how many clusters of individuality can be created. Is there a calm, sunny place for Her, is there a 'den' for Him, is there a two-family scene, and thus one cluster for the Folks and one cluster for the Kids? Do they make things, or collect particular items such as artworks, trophies, memorabilia, books? Having established a physiognomy of these zones of concentration, we must be more inquisitive. The personality of the inhabitants will suggest the degree to which the 'den' is really to be shut away from the rest of the family, or merely to be treated as an open-ended reservation of space. To what extent are the family all as interested as each other in the collection of trophies? In former times architects would not have asked these questions: they would have simply listened to the person who paid for the building. Irrespective of the politics of patronage, we should always try to find out as much as possible about the life to be led in any house that we design. If it is for an unspecified occupant, we should try to write scenarios for the likely people.

The form of the envelope, its apertures and the interaction of inside to outside space may well arise from the grouping of the clusters, augmented by those of bedrooms, the kitchen (and its relation to the main living area) and certainly from our ability to predict the experiencing of the place. Sight-lines from the kitchen to the street, from the 'den' back into the communal areas, from the living space out towards the longest (or most stimulating) outside view: these are predictable. They can be drawn and calculated as the planning of the house proceeds. Such a kinetic and 'experiential' approach need not destroy intentions of order or style or those abstracted mannerisms that mark out architecture from mere organisational planning.

Truss Wall House, Eisaku Ushida and Kathryn Findlay, Tokyo, 1992 (view)

Truss Wall House, Eisaku Ushida and Kathryn Findlay, Tokyo, 1992 (interior)

Soft and Hairy House, Eisaku Ushida and Kathryn Findlay, Tokyo, 1994 (interior)

If the site for the house is more constricted, there are certain design compensations. The consideration of the large plot has enabled us to think of positioning and contriving in a very direct way, related to the occupants. The restricted site may well be narrow, directional, not possessing long views or flanked by the side of the next building. Immediately, a mixture of common sense and the measuring-out of likely components will start to tell you how the building can possibly respond. Perhaps strung along the hard flank wall. Perhaps with the windows all facing the same way. Perhaps with a need to pile things up upon each other. The adoption of a discipline, of directionality or common dimension will be seen as a logical response. For many architects, this will be a welcome imposition for they will have been searching for a series of pegs upon which to hang the more evocative considerations. Why worry about grandfather's habits if he only has a 3 metre-wide sliver of space? His habits will have to constrain themselves! My observation is, however, that far too many architects give up on human and experiential considerations – arguing that pressures of space, or cost or circumstance cannot permit such speculation. In fact, they are too lazy or too doctrinaire to investigate.

As the *a-priori* constraints become tighter, the house may have to depend upon a fairly simple contention: that it can either be very unified or set up two (or possibly three) articulated zones. The 'tight' zone and the 'loose' zone perhaps. The concealed part and the exposed part. The highly serviced part and the 'shed'. The 'romantic' part and the 'bland'. Or whatever. There is no doubt that as the site becomes more extreme, more imploded, more quirky in shape or planning constraints, it starts to take over the creative conversation. A triangular site will set up atmospheric conditions at the first stroke of intervention. A first decision on the location of a services stack, or a double-height space will find the rest of the house dropping-in around. What we are dealing with in all of this, is a choreography of cause and effect (where the points of departure are mandatory) imagination, observation and then – and only then – the minutiae of layout. The better architect is the one who will search for the maximum number of times that these points generate intersections of consequences.

Soft and Hairy House, Eisaku Ushida and Kathryn Findlay, 1994

House, Michael Rotondi, Silverlake, Los Angeles, 1980-86

Aside from this, there is another whole category of endeavour that invigorates the tradition of house design. It stems from a desire to redefine completely the notion of 'house'. Perhaps stemming from the experience of living on board a ship, from the experience of wandering and camping, or perhaps as a part of man's inevitable desire to invent and draw inspiration from territories outside the direct stream (such as painting influenced by mathematics or marketing influenced by theatre), an increasing number of dwellings have been defined as cabins, capsules, pads, pods, nodes or units.

There has also been a concerted move towards the consideration of the 'non-house': the hybrid between home and workplace. Most of these sometimes contradictory notions have arisen from twentieth-century experiences and philosophies. Earlier periods were able to absorb eccentric living into secluded cottages, lodges, turrets or garrets, or simply the uneven use of existing houses. This has become a luxury. Moreover, it is the wish to be both part of metropolitan life and liberated from many of its mundanities that has fuelled the experimental thrust. Economics, too, have pressured the field. Why should a house be so elaborate to build? Why should much of the cost be expended on peripheral features or questionable features such as lofts or garages? Buckminster Fuller asked, 'Why should they weigh so much?'. He then proceeded to develop a series of experimental houses. In parallel was the work of Konrad Wachsmann who devised packages of panel houses. The period of the 1940s and 1950s saw immense activity in this field and, though it was inevitably reacted against by a new bourgeoisie of the 1960s, our reviewed attitudes towards energy and survival revive our interest in these experiments. There are now better, cleaner, lighter materials, more know-how from the aeronautics and space industries and more efficient processing of the traditional materials such as wood, fibre and clay.

Designing an enclosure that contains people sleeping, eating and expressing themselves – and possibly doing things from which they earn money – can be approached from basic principles but not models. Involvement with food does not necessarily mean establishing a kitchen, at least not as a single room or area. Food can be thought of as an availability. We no longer gather around the big

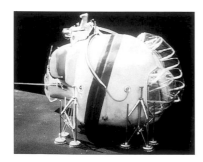

Living Pod, David Greene, 1965

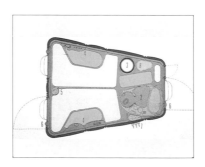

Capsule Homes, Warren Chalk, 1964 (plans)

House at Pacific Palisades, Charles and Ray Eames, Los Angeles, 1949

fireplace in order to keep warm. Many of us can go to sleep in a number of different locations, some of us, on the other hand, enjoy the idea of the bedroom as a private territory and so stake our claim to it with the flag 'bedroom'. Once we think in these terms, the idea of the caravan in a large garden, the thin tented veil over a series of cocoons, the series of trays which open or close within a general space, the possibility of three or four 'food points' or the bathroom-living room are eccentric, but worth consideration.

Technology is also there, waiting to liberate both our thinking and our comfort yet further. The ring main, packaged gas, refrigerated water, lightweight umbrella structures, high insulation quilts, zippers, rolling and sliding devices, heated windows all are waiting for the ingenuity that was anticipated by Chareau's Maison de Verre in Paris of 1929-31, refined and simplified by Charles and Ray Eames' own house at Pacific Palisades of 1949; brought into the world of cybernetics by Ron Herron's 'Robo-House' project of 1989 and now waiting for further input from an energy-aware but digitally-supported generation of designers.

Housing

It has been impossible to avoid the discussion straying from 'the house' into 'housing' since they are, after all, dealing with the same basic need. Yet there are some tricky territories that have to be addressed in knowing how to evaluate the parts, the figurations and (most of all) the psychology of the apartment as distinct from the house. The dream of independence through the possession of a house in a garden – iconographically defined and physically loose from its fellows – has been exploited by politicians, traders and the builders of railways since the 1880s.

The apartment, on the other hand, has an even longer history. The first fortresses were inhabited by a number of different people seeking mutual support. This 'mutuality' versus the house's 'freedom' is an architectural issue. It is underscored by the culture of cities themselves. To be within or without the walls led to a certain tightness or generosity of space (as well as the defensive issue). Inevitably, the European city as it developed systems of servicing – drains, trams and the

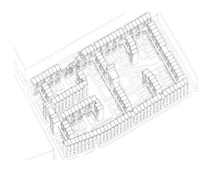

Spangen Housing, Michael Brinkmann, Rotterdam, 1920

Siedlung Bruchfeldstrasse, Ernst May, Frankfurt, 1928

corner *boulangerie* – encouraged a density of building, usually up to six floors above ground and containing courtyards in which support activities and even industry were encouraged. The people within had apartments; there was no question of being a city dweller in an independent structure unless you were very rich. However, Anglo-Saxon and Japanese traditions ran differently. In London and Tokyo apartment buildings are still rare, though actual apartments abound (knitted into buildings that announce themselves as 'houses'). Such cultural quirks need not divert us from the central battle between convenience and personality.

Convenience is the proximity to 'town' and likewise the proximity to maximum servicing; the psychology of the 'en-suite bathroom' which overrides the delights of loose, large space, observed by any discussion with a real-estate agent; the stacking of bathrooms one above the other in a multi-level building, so that the soil stack is direct and efficient. Convenience is the nearness to the elevator from your front door. Personality is rarely taken into consideration in apartment design, yet it is instantly recognisable and valued greatly by some. Of course it can be simulated by the veneer of paintwork, hangings, artefacts or even smells created by the inhabitant. What concerns us here, however, is the possibility that the congealed and surrounded dwelling can be intriguing and memorable.

A frequent configuration for a small apartment is of a narrow reservation of space with a view out at each end. The darkness of the middle is usually resolved by placing the bathroom and the services for the kitchen area. Mechanical ventilation has made such placing possible. Earlier generations of apartments went to great lengths to give the bathroom a window. The modern 'dumb-bell' plan with an environmental release at each end implies a key decision: which end is for living and which for sleeping? In the Lutzowplatz housing of 1990, Christine Hawley and I were presented with a simple answer: with east-west orientation there was the morning sun (and the quiet side) on the east for the bedrooms. The best views, the evening sun and a park could be seen through our attached wintergardens on the west. We were also able to create several double-height living spaces onto this western side. We were determined, however, to avoid wherever possible, the consignment of the person who was cooking or cleaning to a gloomy corner and so the kitchen areas tended to be given prime locations. We also played small tricks with the levels and ceilings so that diagonal views, intriguing glimpses and a variation in floor level could result in seven different types of apartment in a block of only fourteen units.

Irrespective of style, mannerism or tradition, the opportunity of the apartment block is that of balancing out freedom of interpretation (by architect as well as inhabitant) with the necessary logic of entrances, fire escapes, view, orientation, comprehension, noise and comfort. The late nineteenth-century and early twentieth-century apartment buildings should be studied by architects now: they were sometimes extravagant on volume but high on ingenuity. They could also create considerable personality in terms of architectonic space.

The rapid development of Berlin, the wealth and (at last!) urbanisation of London, the intensification of Manhattan, the commodity of the Barcelona grid have all been invested in by apartments that allowed for a fair exercise of personality by the inhabitants. On the one hand, the building itself could be remarkable. The Casa Milá by Gaudi in Barcelona, the courtyard blocks on Berlin's Kurfurstendamm, the mansion blocks flanking the London parks or the towers alongside Central Park in Manhattan use the profiling of the overall form so as to enhance the wit of the internal planning. The Casa Milá takes it further – into the very shaping of the corners and the profile of the wall as it meets the ceiling. Cultural idiosyncrasies give clues to the degrees of contrivance: the English enjoy small-scale events, so you can find many nooks and crannies, small insertions of windows, balconies springing out of other balconies, small rooms tucked into seemingly impossible crevices. A seafaring nation with a liking for the picturesque has certain instincts that have been over-sailed by the international packaged 'flat', but for how long? In Berlin, however, the entrance hall must create a certain doubt as to whether we are entering a palace, a seat of government – or at the very least – a place in which it is impressive to live. The brilliant use of ceiling height and the potential of a variety of ways in which increments of rooms can be created make the Berlin apartments of the turn of the century a memory of civilised city living, as well as a frustration to designers one hundred years later who are constantly reminded of volumetric costing.

The evolution of Le Corbusier's apartments for the Unité d'Habitation at Marseilles (and its successors at Nantes, Berlin and Bruyère) can clearly be traced from his earlier villas and studios. The clarity of intention and wish to create a major released volume is allied to a clever 'locking' of one apartment over and under a corridor that gives two sets of double height in a three-floor increment. His clear iconography of parts and 'stripped-down' aesthetic leaves the inhabitant free to create any number of layers or interferences and so build up his or her personality within. Another key model of public housing stems from the reinterpretation of German Modernist architects of certain English humanitarian models. The publication in of Hermann Muthesius' 'Das Englisches Haus' fed into the cultural logic of the emerging German architecture.

Both countries were inspired by the simultaneous rediscovery of craftsmanship

Casa Milà, Antonio Gaudi, Barcelona, 1906 (elevation)

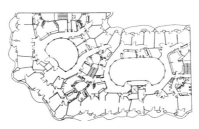

Casa Milà (plan)

Housing at Lutzowplatz, Peter Cook and Christine Hawley, Berlin, 1989-92

and the idea of the factory worker who could once again make contact with trees, home-grown lettuces and a form of 'cottage'. It is no accident that the young Ernst May worked for Parker and Unwin (the designers of many houses in Welwyn Garden City) and later, as City Architect of Frankfurt am Main, he instigated a series of *siedlungen* that had, as a starting point, high standards of bathroom, standard kitchen and gardens. Standard beds and other equipment were also available. The most characteristic of these projects was the Romerberg of 1928 in northern Frankfurt. A riverside site has an inspired section whereby gardens, housing, terraces, vegetable gardens, the public riverside park and the small river form a descending series. This notion of 'riding' the landscape, and of creating terrace and balcony conditions was further developed by the 1950s, 60s and 70s by Atelier 5 of Switzerland, whose work not only inspired their own country but teams of public architects in Scandinavia and England. Simultaneously, there are responses to a number of coveted ideals: the relative individualism or 'identity' of the apartment, the implication of 'groundedness', the reminiscence of landscape, and the creation of a relatively large proportion of external surface.

Another paradox is thus exposed. For just as the twentieth-century interpretations of the nineteenth-century mansion blocks were able to take advantage of better plumbing and better electrics, there is a reversion away from the 'tight' city. Le Corbusier himself lays great stress on the existence of the external garden: in one of May's Frankfurt *siedlungen* (at Sachsenhousen West) there are parallel strips of public garden, each planted with a distinctive tree type.

Once the six-floor (or more) vertical slab of apartments is loosened away, it would seem that many creative architects resort to a polarised separation of ideas. The external balcony was consigned from its high symbolic role in the 1930s to that of optional appendage. How could it compete with the setback terrace? It was felt that the profile of the blocks themselves should relish in their economy of space and economy of means. The tower block (for a while) became more symbolically desirable than the strip. It could pack a series of four, six or eight apartments around a stack. Strange indentations of surface or deliberately individual plan forms were both expensive and irrational.

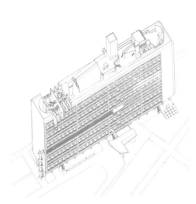

Unité d'Habitation, Le Corbusier, Marseilles, 1948

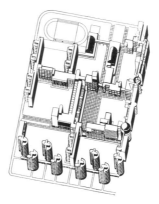

Study Community, I Kuzmin, 1929 (project)

The Frankfurt Bed, designed in association with the Frankfurt Siedlungen in the late 1920s

Meanwhile, the ground-hugging developments began to be rationalised into that inevitable hybrid, the 'quasi-villa'. Borrowing from the remembered bourgeois model, and reminded by the fact that in so many cities, villas are converted into several apartments, architects were encouraged to build small and independent blocks. In the IBA programme of the 1980s some good architects found themselves trapped in this way, but were able to wear their stylistic character on the face of often commonplace flat planning. Contrasting this with the previous *bauaustellung*; the Hansaviertel of 1956 is not just a question of architectural philosophies but of the value given to the living space. The Hansa blocks are almost all the externalisation of planning in which great faith had clearly been placed. The inevitable issue of designing inside-to-out or outside-to-in is thus faced head on. It is best to pursue the design of multiple housing with two drawings unfurling simultaneously. On the one hand, the general mass and organisation of the block becomes progressively more clear, more clever or at least more assured; on the other, those stages push, pull and visually clarify the internal spaces. A constant feedback from the one to the other is the essential process.

Certain artificial patterning can be stimulated: the quasi-villas might optimise around eight, twelve or eighteen units, a terrace might optimise around twenty (four units: four per landing six floors high). In the 1930s there were optimal groupings based upon the now extinct significance of the laundry or upon the catchment area of a small school. In some ways it is for the designer to invent a significance that may be logically parallel to defining how many angels can sit on a pin! Once again we have hit that zone of paradox and hyperbole in which the creative trigger of architecture is recharged by calling attention to a significant measure, or significant focus, parallel no doubt to a composer rationalising the choice of the key 'D' for playing out an essay in sonata form.

To what extent the inhabitants need to be reminded of their coerced state depends upon the arrogance or sensitivity of the designer. It is, for instance, possible to create a 'secret' conglomerate. By passing the general circulation past a series of architectural decoys or 'events', by distorting the physical announcement of landings, entrances, external spaces, balconies and roofs you

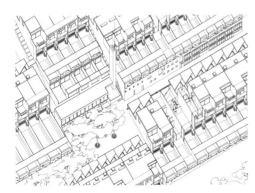

Hallen Housing, Atelier 5, near Berne, 1955-61 (diagram)

Housing at Hansaviertel, Walter Gropius, Berlin, 1952

141

can pretend (by designing) that the building is some mysterious and continuous world. Alternatively, you can make great play of the particular elevator shaft around which twenty lucky apartments foregather. It can be coloured green and its users branded as some conglomerate just two steps removed from a netball team. Whether this really causes them pleasure or embarrassment melts away in the light of the resulting architectural statement. In other words, we should be both inventive and knowing in our choice of rhetorical features. The English are suspicious of conglomerates, so perhaps they need the decoy of variation the most. Other cultures may or may not be attracted by the idea of anonymity. Certain cultures are waiting for the architecture to offer them the chance to lean over the garden fence and gossip, to sit out on the porch and nod to the passing neighbour; to peer from behind a lace curtain – noting who it is that comes and goes. In Oslo, a city with cheap electricity, the owners of apartments leave their curtains open and their lights on. There is infrequent movement within, but their style and literacy (the Norwegians have many books) is demonstrated to the passer-by. Modern housing can rightly be accused of disregarding these societal traits. It should be possible for the designer to both note them and provide for them without parody – and without imitating the precise historical devices involved.

To want to be loved, respected, noticed or left alone: to want to physically or symbolically engage with cohabitants or neighbours is pretty basic. But what are the appropriate physical devices involved? The fire-run, sun direction and optimum density are acknowledged generators of housing design. We can, however, overlay some new generators. Respect could be checked against our sets of formal elements and domestic icons, all of which affect the size of door as well as size of terrace, accessibility of window, curvature of ceiling, brightness of kitchen area, location of the dog and innumerable other features. Love could be responded to by surface, form, 'specialness', independence and very subtle positioning of the loved-one's domain (or favourite elements). Being noticed is probably a little more general and detached, but certainly important in the design of a dwelling. The symbols of identity are to be carefully chosen. Privacy might seem the most obvious and simply requires a closed room, but it may also be at one end of a

Ocean liner design, Norman Bel Geddes, 1932

Tokyo Forum, Neil Denari, 1989 (project)

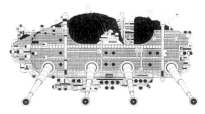

Walking City, Ron Herron, 1964

scale of conditions: private; slightly exposed; fully exposed; overt; prominent; and more to do with location than form. Incidentally, there can be parallel scales of noise or light quality, of traditional domesticity or comfort.

Castles, Hotels, Clubs or Ships

With the exception of hotels, this group may seem *passé* as a category for the discussion of buildings for the twenty-first century. Yet one needs to reintroduce this special category of building due to the issue of interdependence. I will refer to the castle, once again, as the generic model. The defensive part (bastions, walls, turrets and moat) were the *a-priori* elements but the keep, sheds, dungeons, stores, workshops and dwelling places that nestled within, were its sustenance. The hotel is not so different. First it needs guests. After that the guests need to be sustained and amused. More subtly, the hotel very often needs a reason for being there, mere location not neccesarily being sufficient. This may be stimulated by encouraging and facilitating conferences. Now we have a hybrid; a self-generating miniature city. The cruise ship is similar, only dependent upon location in the general sense. The club exists to offer itself primarily as a meeting place, but may become a virtual city for the gaming addict or the elitist member who enjoys its existence as a discriminate village existing in the centre of an indiscriminate city.

All the above seem at first to be enjoyable temporary accommodation. After the battle, the vacation, the voyage or the session, it is assumed that we go home to a house, flat or cottage. On the other hand, more and more people are irritated with commuting, are extending holidays, are demanding facilities or services in or near the home. More and more people eat in restaurants. The mall in Houston is several blocks long. The underground 'cities' in Tokyo and Montreal cause a subtle breakdown of the independence of the city building, as do skywalks. The real implication of all this is for us to consider a generically new building type which is hinted at and prepared for by these existing models, but which is, in its way, as radical as the first apartment block or the first shopping mall. The city in a single building? Perhaps. The hybrid between apartment house and hotel? Perhaps. The cruise ship (with all its distractions and interdependence of parts) wrapped into a highly distinctive and complete form? Perhaps. More clubs for everyday people (with live-in accommodation)? Perhaps.

Public housing has become an issue avoided by politicians and associated in the public mind with regimentation, yet the desire to live deep in the city persists. In parallel, the desire for really good city-level servicing and human interaction also persists – but is it in the minds of those who enjoy the tranquility of the countryside or the release of suburbia? If so, then we need to create some hybrids: city blocks without the city; the beached ship; the ability to work in or very near to the home with something more than the table-top terminal. New levels of health and sporting facilities, helipads and crèches and places of escape will be needed. Organisationally, circulation will be both ostentatious and discrete, with several kinds of spatial experience. Moreover, unlike the old city 'block' and 'mall', constant revision will be required.

BEYOND THE RULES

This chapter offers a selection of ten buildings that transcend the simple manners of architecture. The true spirit of design is a force that goes beyond merely satisfying the demands for space and performance yet at the same time is one that is able to take formal, spatial and technical initiatives. The following ten buildings have little in common with each other except, for me, a distinct memorability achieved at a variety of times, though predominantly in the twentieth century. I have deliberately not related their description to any categories that I might have used earlier, though an amusing game might be constructed by codifying them later.

NORWICH CATHEDRAL
Norwich

A heavy stone cathedral constructed in the eleventh, twelfth and thirteenth centuries and standing 140 metres long and with a tall, delicate spire might seem an odd choice to send out messages to the design of one thousand years later. Even to admirers of English cathedrals it is not a classic case, for it is influenced by French Norman planning at its eastern end (with the semicircular ambulatory and *appendagèsque* chapels). It appeals to he who seeks calm, yet discovers dramatic or virtuoso episodes within.

The process of adding a clerestory to the basic Norman structure more than two hundred years later and adding the vaulting one hundred years later still, creates a combined effort that belies the advances of technique over that time. If the Norman columns and arching seem a little beefy, they are clothed on the outside by aisles of the lighter (but still fairly 'correct')

Perpendicular period. A building such as this can therefore be regarded as a laying on or adding on of parts, with essential ground formulae firmly established. The cloister, for example, is a later addition from the thirteenth to the fifteenth centuries and makes for an extremely relaxed insertion into the figure of the main cathedral form. Looking at the diagram produced by the cathedral buildings, at various refectories and infirmaries, schools and the walled area of the cathedral close with its three memorable gate structures, one senses an architecture of continual composition. Some of it is created from the original elements, some of it geometrically consistent with that, but added piecemeal. Then, once the enclave is created, a series of looser but calmly complementary buildings are encouraged to develop.

The mannerisms of the buildings range from the heroic (the flying buttresses around the east end of the Cathedral and the spire), the knowing and the elegant, through to the modest incursion into the corner of a cloister wall. Craft merges into invention wherever you look. There are high-level galleries of an unusually early date. In the chancel, there is recourse to a series of geometries layered one over the other. There are changes of mannerisms folded into the apparent continuity of the nave on the fifth pier east of the crossing. There are elaborate compositions of tracery and shafts and gables, even around the cloister; powerful form and detail even on the gates to the Cathedral close. The issue raised by this assemblage is that of continuity and the existence of a powerful initial thrust (the system of the cathedral formula) that enables almost endless addition and revision (within limits of respect and material). There is a Classicism of manners which exists in this very non-Classical building.

HAMAR BISPEGAARD MUSEUM

Norway, 1967-73
Sverre Fehn

The building is a combination of parts of the shell and remains of the medieval Bishop's Manor which have then been infiltrated by a very dynamic route and other insertions. In Fehn's own words: 'the concept has been developed of a *suspend museum* which will make it possible to get a grasp on history, not by means of pages in a book written in ink – but as it emerges in the world of archaeology'. For much of its trajectory, the path is above ground and weaves through changes in geometry and glances past inserted objects with great dexterity.

The first move in the sequence is sheer virtuosity: the ramp starts in the yard of the 'U'-shaped monument and performs a near-hairpin turn before violating the corner of the building. Once inside, it gives onto a platform on one side and a spiral stair on the other. With extraordinary nonchalance, the platform reveals itself to be the top of descending auditorium terracing. In the other direction, the ramp (which has now become a bridge) cuts through the middle of the contained space. Its very directness is almost shocking, and at the same time acts as a necessary foil, in addition to making constant reference to the collection of sequences that are lined by crumbling ruins.

Openings are retained in the state that they had reached in the late 1960s: simply being skimmed over by plate glass. Similarly, the pits and recesses that are visible down from the bridge and ramp are either left exposed or skinned in glass. The experience of space and remnants is essentially panoramic – from above as well as alongside. The wing of the building that is more specifically used as a folk museum is more formally infiltrated with screen walls and exquisitely well-considered hanging and lighting devices. Here, Fehn's closeness to the Italian methods of Carlo Scarpa and others is traceable. Along with this, however, is a clearly developed understanding of light control – a theme he developed through to his much later Ice Museum.

In all of Fehn's work there is a combination of simple and clear intent, a quiet formal vocabulary and a confidence that allows moments of great audacity. In a culture that requires us to honour, preserve and use old buildings, without insulting them by mere imitation, we should study buildings such as the Hamar Museum with its sensitive, contrapuntal action and the twist of the surgeon's knife. It is also essentially theatrical in its unfolding of space through procession and a deft understanding of light.

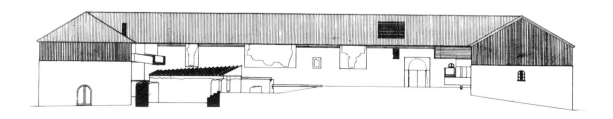

LLOYDS BANK

Buenos Aires, 1960-66
Clorindo Testa

Though very much of its time, this building still presents an extraordinarily powerful face to the observer. Its facades, or rather, the outer layering of screens and glass walls, filter out a large internal space that is dextrously infilled by a series of trays and floors. Very solid substances, such as concrete, are carved boldly, and impeccably constructed and finished. Yet the most intriguing feature of this building is its evacuated outer corner and the large, remorseless 'eyelid' of concrete that hangs down over this corner space.

The concept is of a large building inserted into a very tight street intersection in the business quarter of Buenos Aires, for those inside the building, it presents a sense of released space. The buildings on the opposite corners of the street are seen through the layers of apertured concrete and inner glass screens by way of light that is shaded by the 'eyelid' in such a way that they appear to form a great outer room.

Meanwhile, the inner spaces are heroic: the trays of circulation run boldly, in line with the outer layers but some considerable distance within. Thus a 'banking hall' is created, but not as a simplistic box of space. The major elements are thick, bold, directional and sculpturally assured, yet the whole has been aptly described as 'Piranesi-like' in its ability to convey a sense of surprise and an agglomeration of nearly-hidden spaces.

As with Sverre Fehn, this architect relies upon a relatively small vocabulary of preferred forms but is able to create out of them a building of ever-unfolding spatial quality. Bold elements do not just stand there as figures, but almost as foils to the mysterious territories and profiles that they frame. Such qualities are visible both from the inside and by peering in from the street. Concrete is used plastically, glass is used simply, suspended structure is used as necessary, but not as a fetish.

VITRA FURNITURE MUSEUM
Weil am Rheim, Germany, 1989
Frank O Gehry

This is unashamedly a showpiece building most often discussed in architectural circles as a brilliant but curious cultural hybrid. Here, the argument goes, is Frank Gehry – the apocryphal Californian architect from Los Angeles, who has made a virtue of dexterity in stud-framing, board, chain metal fencing and hard sun but now performs here in Germany, absorbing the culture and continuity of European craftsmanship and their serious attitude towards design. Is he not mocking Europe? Is he not making a toy? Is he not working in concrete but thinking in cardboard? It is as if the tightness and ponderousness of so much European thinking has to be addressed by this virtuoso and most highly-informed designer.

Those who carp seem to ignore the mastery of space and directness of plan. They seem incapable of crediting the experience as going beyond local culture and a self-conscious position, but nonetheless deem it a highly intelligent design. The building reminds us of essentials; of the degree to which entry can be treated as a total and disassociative process. So, the entrance captures the wind and reinvents our referencing system. The chambers within play with the establishment of a (generally orthogonal) system and then make such an array of overlays upon it that we might believe ourselves to be back in late Gothic or Rococo situations. But here they manifest at such a bold and basic scale: light comes in and is then shafted in a number of different 'theatrical' directions; figuration is there, but often only to be registered as bold shadows on clear flanks of white, interior surface.

The essentials are of formal parts defining the full manifestation. A wall really does define space, a shaft really does connect the sky and a ceiling inclination really does change the atmosphere of the enclosing space. As with the Purist Modernism of the 1920s, there is a minimum of interference by details, surfaces and colour. But unlike much Purist architecture this work is not afraid of creative adrenaline, which probably explains its incomprehensibility to many Swiss or German critics. To the student of figure-to-form, the Vitra Museum is unsurpassed.

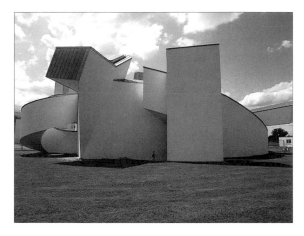 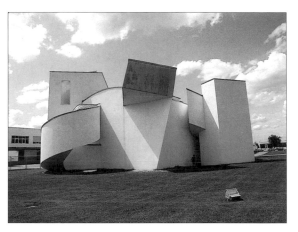

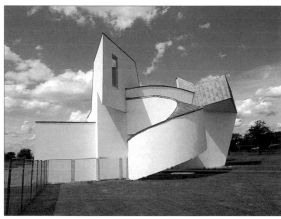 

YALE CENTRE FOR BRITISH ART
New Haven, Connecticut, 1969-74
Louis I Kahn

A rich university with a powerful architectural tradition attracts rhetorical objects, so the architectural collector has a choice of two Kahn buildings. In some ways, the Yale Centre for British Art has a more relaxed role in any discussion of his work. Unlike the Yale University Art Gallery which eighteen years earlier established Kahn as a prestige architect, the centre is not inherently concerned with structure or primary elements. Indeed, it is remarkably calm and presents itself to the surrounding streets as a well-ordered container. The regular stone-faced frame is of a dimension that could be found in any downtown area in the latter half of the twentieth century. On closer inspection, there is a range of more imaginative placing of windows than is usual; the tonal quality of the opaque panels succeeds in a game that has often been attempted in modern architecture to present grey panels and windows alongside within a dominant frame in order to create the idea of continuity. All too often this fails. Here the balance and the detailing plus the range of placement has succeeded.

This is often regarded as a conservative work in relation to Kahn's other public buildings, and the plan presents a parallel discipline to that of the elevation. A grid of approximately 7 metres is set up and continued throughout. It is never evacuated for more than two bays and the largest inserted form is no more than 9 metres (a circular stair drum). Indeed, there are few eccentric insertions of any kind. The building is ten bays long and six bays wide. Two 'court' conditions are carved out from the centre two bays. On the one side a larger evacuation of space and on the other a smaller (only 14 x 14 metres). A discreet sunken garden and shop are the only peripheral elements. British art is itself not noted for high drama and to surprise you with its inner power, I have deliberately continued this brief introduction in straight, dull, passive terms because that is the way of both the building (and the tradition of the art that it contains). This building understands light and repose supremely well. There are cuts into the predictable panelling of the court walls that give piquancy to this sedate and episodic art. Indeed, it is the quality of episode seen against strong calmness that is most memorable. Kahn, like Lewerentz, knew just when to pull out the stops and probably enjoyed the idea of tantalisation.

TOWER OF THE WINDS
Yokohama , 1986
Toyo Ito

Emerging from Yokohama station you come upon the usual downtown cacophony of bus shelters and street furniture incarcerated by an undistinguished selection of high buildings. Suddenly Ito's tower is there, like an unexpected breeze of calm in sea of chaos. It is only 21 metres high and oval in plan form. The lowest part is cut away to line with some low (and unmemorable) housing for equipment. It is only the shaft itself that registers. By day it is elegant. By night it is stunning.

The film of the surface is of perforated aluminium (not unlike several of his other works). Behind this, however, come a number of layers. Acrylic mirror plates, 1,280 mini-lamps and twelve white rings of neon which are programmed to respond to the quantity of noise outside as well as to the wind velocity and direction. In Ito's words: 'It is controlled as if it were environmental music . . . on occasion, the aluminium panels become an almost transparent film, but at times the panels "rise to the surface" in the flood light'.

In other Ito pieces, such as the Nomad restaurant (now defunct) and an exhibition at the Victoria and Albert Museum in London, the interplay of programming and shimmering layers create an almost ethereal architecture that would have been impossible in earlier times and suggest that he is certainly a creative pioneer. He is one of the most seductive makers of surround and this small tower is not just some small gizmo-architecture, but a prototype for one of his more urban-scaled projects which is hinted at by his Paris library.

Imitations of Ito's work always fall into the trap of inserting too much surface form, and it is his ability to discriminate and design only towards what is comprehended by the eye that makes his work so original.

GLIENICKE PALACE AND GARDEN BUILDINGS
Berlin , 1824-37
Karl Friedrich Schinkel

Without consciously weighing the portentous aspects of Schinkel's work, without carrying the foreknowledge of his abilities elsewhere (the Neue Wache, the temples, the Altes Museum) one can simply arrive at the Glienicke gardens and delight in the crisp elegance of the buildings and the focused placing both in terms of location, sequence and view.

By this time, a mature architect who has such a clear of parts that, to my eye, relate to Swedish Neoclassicism (the historical reality being the reverse of course: Asplund and Lewerentz shared the same copy of a Schinkel book, which was transported between them by a man with a big bicycle-basket!). Yet Schinkel had himself avidly consumed the Gothic, the Egyptian and the English landscape gardeners Brown, Repton and Loudon. The

intriguing aspect of this mixture is to be found in the first Glienicke insertion for Prince Karl of Prussia (there had been an eighteenth-century resort on the site). Ostensibly a billiard hall, the Casino faces the lake and establishes an infiltrated embankment of trellised architecture. Detail is layered in, becoming more intimate as it becomes closer to the windows and culminating in the detail of the interior. Natural growth is encouraged at the edges, but unlike some English parallels, it is not totally encouraged to creep around the inserted parts. It is this essentially urbane character of the park that is fascinating.

The palace itself is modest and succeeds in presenting itself as a simple structure (such as that found in the environs of a large estate) rather than being a 'main'

building. The stripped surfaces of Schinkel's work contribute to such a mood. The subsequent growth of the wooded landscape supplies the necessary foil to this theatre of the modest; again, a far more urbane move than presenting us with a fragment of a large building, or a scaled-down (but complicated) implant. The large belvedere, however, reminds us that Schinkel was able to use Glienicke as a testbed for his most refined crafting and composition.

Berlin is an essential repository of developed architecture, particularly of the nineteenth and twentieth centuries. If nothing else these gardens provide respite from a hot city. The essential requirement is, however, to sit long and muse hard upon the degree to which calculation, refinement and repose can be part of the same objective.

GOTHENBURG LAW COURTS
Gothenburg , 934-37
Gunnar Asplund

Much has been written about this building as a sensitive addition to an existing Classical structure, and surely the history of its progress, from a competition-winning scheme in 1935 to the combined structure of 1937, would make fascinating reading. My own reaction to the new part is, however, as that of someone engaged by a piece of new architecture.

Three sides of a courtyard are formed by the original building, which is solid, and the fourth is the glass wall of the new wing. Behind this glass is a wide stair leading up to the courtroom level. The stair sits into a plate that itself reads as a bridge. Within the new building is an atrium, and two of the courts sit deep behind this. A close look at plan and section reveals a strategy of gradually increasing voluptuousness as one works sideways away from the old building and moves upwards

away from the ground. Indeed, the section is far from being an orthodox simple modern figure. There is evidence of Asplund's 'honing' away procedure (noticeable in almost all his work) so that the quality of light and view and profile work together – and to hell with the drawn figure!

My own generation of English architects was surrounded by poor copies of Asplund's architecture. Sweden was the preferred Social Modernist stomping-ground for our teachers. English provincial towns sprouted concrete stairs and hanging clocks that were immediately recognisable from poor photographs of the Gothenburg building.

Never be put off by poor imitations or features or figurations. If at all possible, go and see the buildings. There is no substitute. I was hardly expecting the quality of joyous release from

the Classicism of the old building – the great sense of space and lightness, perhaps a reminder of what the space inside Asplund's Paradise Restaurant at the 1930 Stockholm exhibition might have been like. I was unprepared for the sexy profiling and the texture of the columns. I realised that every copy of the staircase and clock had 'got it wrong' (usually by being too lumpy and too thick). I was unprepared for the impact of generous plywood casing and the impact that skilfully placed and deliciously shaped curved rooms could have in the context of a rectilinear building.

A building such as this makes you very aware of shape; not just as profile, but shape as applied to evacuated space, to the degree roundness of an edge and then, by the same token, the profiling of a column, a handrail or a lamp.

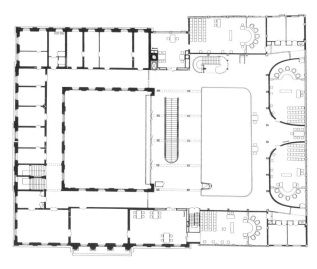

NATIONAL TRAINING CENTRE FOR RHYTHMIC GYMNASTICS
Alicante, Spain, 1992
Enric Miralles

What can possibly generate a building such as this? Surely not rules or systems or procedures. What type of organisation is it? What manner of architecture are we looking at? Is it Structuralism or Modernism, sculpture or engineering? Is it not an expressionistic virtuoso piece?

The National Training Centre for Rhythmic Gymnastics is thus an ideal end piece for a book about the design of architecture; Miralles is one of the most fluent and best informed of his generation. His own heroes are Le Corbusier and Louis Kahn. Prior to this work, he has proved to be a brilliant manipulator of objects in free space. He can imagine and generate a run of flowing material high up in the sky which then seems to be 'draped' with fabric in free-range clusters. Miralles is quite sure-footed about paths and diagonal runs of stairs or ramps.

The plan of the Alicante building seems to gather the sinews of the outstretched arms and draw them along the 'trunk' of the building. As with Norwich Cathedral, the large rectilinear enclosure (then a cloister, now an arena) is tucked, entirely consequentially, under the arm. The constructed parts of the building seem to have a self-contained character, as if they are complete toys made from a construction kit and able to run around the site. But then, partly drawn by the imaginary 'force-field' of the building, they begin to hover nearer and nearer to each other. Suddenly, there is an electricity as some corners come into proximity or contact. My imagined dynamics are prompted by the extreme conceptual brilliance coupled with the compositional 'lightness' (and sometimes physical lightness) of the whole thing. Unlike some of the other buildings in this chapter, the building at Alicante is full of its own form and parts. Miralles enjoys the putting together of the building. He is a real 'maker', far too fast and brilliant in his abilities to stop and worry about the proposition of 'rightness' in abstracted terms. In analytical terms, he can explain every move.

PETRI CHURCH, KLIPPAN
Sweden
Sigurd Lewerentz

A disarmingly modest group of buildings on the edge of a small town in southern Sweden send out few clues as to the intensity of the interior of the church. Even the bell tower looks very little more than a domestic chimney stack. An 'L'-shaped run of offices, confirmation room and parish hall wrap around and shelter the church building. Shallow pitched roofs are sufficient for the supporting parts and very slight barrel-vaults are given to roof the church. Closer inspection of the exterior reveals the presence of small or horizontally thin windows in clusters that each have their own mannerism. It also reveals the quite idiosyncratic way in which the modest walls of the entrance are drawn up into a series of small, bent shafts. Be it drainage channels or stairs, there is intricacy throughout.

Those who already know Lewerentz's Resurrection Chapel in Stockholm or his St Mark's Church in Bjorkhagen will enter the building less surprised than others, but will still undoubtedly be affected by the sheer intimacy of the extraordinary light control within. The twisted shafts are bringing in mere slivers of sharp light down upon modest spaces that are immediately special without the need for any other architectural heroics. The church itself is minimally detailed without door frames or skirtings. There are windows which create a very close relationship between the body of the room itself and the weather or atmosphere of the outside landscape. It is a dark room with an undulating floor and occasional cuts into it such as the font.

Apparently, Lewerentz (who was already in his late seventies) made adjustments to the detailed design of each room as he went along supervising in order to tune up the individual atmosphere of the parts of the building. In the end, this is work for the connoisseur almost impossible to categorise or to pin to a date; minimalist in its avoidance of rhetoric but hardly minimalist in its search for the evocative and the romantic; nordic in its valuation of light, but tougher than many northern buildings.

POSTSCRIPT

Almost all the buildings in this personal, rather random
survey seem to prompt me to talk about light, space, energy
or theatrics. Perhaps these are the most difficult aspects of
design to capture and almost certainly the most difficult to
do. Small confusions of mannerism will disappear if you look
hard and begin to enjoy the architecture. Allow yourself to
wallow in the cumulative power of one idea leading to
another . . . and onward to the next.